Editor
Leasha Taggart, M.A. Ed.

Managing Editor
Karen J. Goldfluss, M.S. Ed.

Editor-in-Chief
Sharon Coan, M.S. Ed.

Illustrators
Blanca Apodaca
Ken Tunell

Interior Art Concepts
Ann Barnell

Art Coordinator
Denice Adorno

Cover Art
Barb Lorseyedi

Product Manager
Phil Garcia

Imaging
Alfred Lau
Rosa C. See

Publisher
Mary D. Smith, M.S. Ed.

Authors

Jane Routte & Ann Barnell

Teacher Created Resources, Inc.
6421 Industry Way
Westminster, CA 92683
www.teachercreated.com

ISBN-0-7439-3093-2

©2001 Teacher Created Resources, Inc.
Reprinted, 2006
Made in U.S.A.

Table of Contents

Welcome to Mexico

Mexico is a country of wonderful and varied delights. It is a country full of color, history, and excitement. The land and the people of Mexico are as varied as anywhere else on earth. It is a country of blended cultures and traditions. The great wonder of Mexico is its diversity. There is no such thing as a "typical" Mexican person, food, or tradition, as all of these vary greatly from area to area and time to time. Through the activities and experiences presented in this book, your students will grow in their appreciation of this exciting country.

Mexico's history is an exciting one. It was the home of the great Olmec, Toltec, Mayan, and Aztec cultures, to name only a few. These native tribes built large cities with great pyramids and complicated social systems. The Mayans developed mathematical systems which rivaled anything in Europe, developed the concept of zero in math, and were the best astronomers of the time. The calendars of these great tribes were amazingly accurate with the solar and lunar years. When the conquistadors came to Mexico in 1521, they found the Aztec city of Tenochtitlán (later Mexico City) to be larger than any of the great cities of Europe at that time. The descendents of these powerful tribes are still an active and proud factor in the social climate of Mexico.

Since the Spanish conquest, Mexican history has been one of strife and struggle. Revolution and political turmoil are the landmarks of Mexico's past, but along with that are the great artists, writers, and leaders who came from this country of contrasts. The mixture of the Spanish culture with the native Indian cultures has created a country of great diversity and color. Today Mexico is making itself known as a growing industrial force and as a highly regarded destination for tourists of the world.

Tourists are attracted to the long Pacific coastline and to the beautiful beaches along the Gulf of Mexico and the Caribbean Sea. The inland areas of Mexico are attractive for their mountains and beautiful vegetation. Many tourists also visit the extensive archaeological sites that are scattered throughout the country. The rugged mountains that run down the western edge of the high plateau offer outstanding views and are home to the famous Copper Canyon, a canyon wider, longer, and deeper than the Grand Canyon.

Mexico's colorful traditions capture the heart and the imagination. Music and dancing are a daily part of life in Mexican towns and cities. Traditional dancing costumes represent the various areas of the country, each with its colorful signature appearance. The music of the country is varied and ranges from heartfelt ballads of love to music that makes feet dance wildly.

Welcome to Mexico *(cont.)*

Mexico's food is famous for its piquant taste. Hot chilies, tamales, tacos, and enchiladas are only the most well known of the tasty food of Mexico. The variety of foods and tastes are as varied as the people and the land. The traditional Indian dishes have mixed with the cuisine of the Spanish to create a unique and pleasing food experience.

Piñatas, fiestas, fireworks, and food are wonderful parts of the complex culture of Mexico. But Mexico is also a country plagued by problems of poverty, illiteracy, and ancient struggles of social classes. Spanish is the recognized official language, but there are 56 different Indian groups and many different languages spoken in Mexico. For many of these people, Spanish is a second language. Poverty is a problem in much of the country as Mexico's government races to keep up with the other nations. The country spends twice as much on education as it does on defense and has made great inroads into the illiteracy problem in recent years.

We know that your students will enjoy their journey into Mexico through the activities in this book. Activities presented in this book have been classroom tested and are carefully chosen to help the busy teacher. We recommend that you use the mercado as your culminating activity, as it gives the class a chance to bring many of their projects and experiences together. It also provides an opportunity for the students to demonstrate their knowledge to other students, parents, and the community. However you choose to use this book, we know that your students will develop a life-long interest in the fascinating country of Mexico.

4

Interesting Facts About Mexico

Official name: Estados Unidos de Mexico (United States of Mexico)

Capital: Mexico City is among the largest cities in the world with the estimates for the metropolitan area reaching as high as 23,000,000. It is usually considered second in size after Tokyo, but statistics vary.

National Anthem: "Himno Nacional Mexicano"

Area: 761,403 square miles (close to three times the size of Texas)

Coastlines: 4,558 miles of Pacific coastline and 1,743 miles of coastline along the Gulf of Mexico and the Caribbean

Population: Approximately 95,200,000 people reside in Mexico, the country with the largest Spanish-speaking population in the world. Mexico is ranked approximately eleventh in the world population totals.

Constitution: In 1824, Mexico's first constitution established the country as a federal republic. The first elected president was Guadalupe Victoria.

Highest mountain: Pico de Orizaba. This mountain is the third highest mountain in North America (after Mount McKinley and Mount Logan). It is 5,747 meters or 18,855 feet. It is in the state of Veracruz.

Mexico's art: Mexico is famous for its arts and handicrafts. Although many of the arts are available throughout the country, some states are particularly famous for their specialties.

Glassware: Oaxaca, Puebla, Jalisco
Woodwork: Sonora, Michoacán, Morelos
Pottery: Oaxaca, Puebla, Guerrero, Jalisco
Textiles: Chiapas, Oaxaca, Puebla, Coahuila, Nayarit
Jewelry and metalwork: Guerrero, Querétaro, Michoacán
Hammocks: Yucatán, Campeche, Michoacán
Leather: Zacatecas, León, Jalisco, Michoacán
Lacquerware: Michoacán, Guerrero, Chiapas

Directory for the World Wide Web

These sites have interesting information about Mexico, the people, and the traditions. There are many more sites with helpful information, and new ones are constantly developing. Use your Web browsers to find more.

http://birch.palni.edu/~hispanic/
http://www.mesoweb.com/
http://www.inegi.gob.mx/difusion/ingles/portadai.html
http://www.go2mexico.com/
http://www.library.csustan.edu/lboyer/modern_languages/mexican.html
http://www.indigenouspeople.org/natlit/natlit.htm
http://members.xoom.com/_XOOM/IndigLit/origins.htm
http://www.geocities.com/Paris/Bistro/7445/spanish.html
http://www.azcentral.com/ent/dead/
http://www.mexweb.com/muertos.htm
http://www.in-forum.com/specials/dec/guadalupe/
http://www.geocities.com/holidayzone/cinco/index.html
http://www.mexonline.com/index.html-ssi
http://webdemexico.com.mx/
http://www.californiamall.com/holidaytraditions/traditions-mexico.htm
http://www.mexconnect.com/
http://mexico-travel.com/fiestas/fiestas.html
http://nosc.mil/planet_earth/countries/mexico.htm.
http://bertha.pomona.claremont.edu.cslo/mcushman/final.html
http://gaia.ecs.csus.edu/~arellano/index.html
http://www.mipaisimports.com/index.html
http://www.milagrosseattle.com/
http://www.milagrosgallery.com/index.html
http://www.crizmac.com/index.html

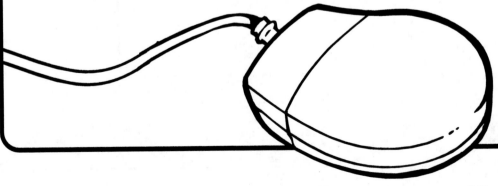

Bibliography

Ancona, George. *Fiesta Fireworks*. Lothrop, Lee & Shepherd, 1998.

Ancona, George. *Pablo Remembers the Day of the Dead*. Lothrop, Lee & Shepherd, 1991.

Beck, Veer. *Beaker's Mexico*. Prentice Hall, 1993.

Brooke, Virginia. *Piñatas*. Abington Press, 1966.

Burns, Roxanne. *How the Aztecs Lived*. Monarca, 1999.

Burns, Roxanne. *How the Maya Lived*. Monarca, 1999.

Caldecott, Barrio. *Paper Mâché*. Franklin Watts, 1992.

Czernecki, Stefan. *The Hummingbird's Gift*. Hyperion, 1994.

Delacre, Lulu. *Arroz con Leche: Popular Songs and Rhymes from Latin America*. Scholastic, 1989.

de Paola, Tomie. *The Lady of Guadalupe*. Holiday House, 1980.

de Paola, Tomie. *The Legend of the Poinsettia*. Putnam's, 1994.

de Paola, Tomie. *The Tale of Rabbit and Coyote*. Putnam's, 1994.

England, Tamara. *Josefina's Craft Book*. Pleasant Company, 1998.

Fiesta Mexico. Grolier Educational, 1997.

Ganeri, Anita. *Mexico*. Franklin Watts, 1994.

Gavin, Jamila. *Our Favorite Stories*. DK, 1997.

González, Lucia M. *Señor Cat's Romance and Other Favorite Stories from Latin America*. Scholastic, 1997.

Grossman, Patricia. *Saturday Market*. Lothrop, Lee and Shepherd, 1994.

Guy, Ginger Foglesong. *Fiesta!* Greenwillow Books, 1996.

Hall, Nancy Abraham. *The Baby Chicks Sing*. Little, Brown and Co., 1994.

Haskins, James. *Count Your Way Through Mexico*. Carolrhoda Books, 1989.

Hewitt, Sally. *The Aztecs*. Children's Press, 1996.

Illsley, Linda. *A Taste of Mexico*. Raintree Steck-Vaughn, 1995.

Irizarry, Carmen. *Passport to Mexico*. Franklin Watts, 1994.

Jermyn, Leslie. *Welcome to Mexico*. Gareth Stevens, 1999.

Kalman, Bobbie. *Mexico, the Culture*. Crabtree, 1993.

Kalman, Bobbie. *Mexico, the Land*. Crabtree, 1993.

Kalman, Bobbie. *Mexico, the People*. Crabtree, 1993.

Klepper, Nancy. *Our Global Village—Mexico*. Milliken, 1990.

Bibliograpy *(cont.)*

"Land of the Feathered Serpent." Map. National Geographic Society, 1968.

"Land of the Maya." Map. National Geographic Society, 1989.

Lowell, Susan. *The Three Little Javelinas*. Northland, 1992.

Luenn, Nancy. *A Gift for Abuelita*. Rising Moon, 1998.

Marcus, Rebecca. *Fiesta Time in Mexico*. Garrard, 1974.

McDonald, Fiona. *How Would You Survive as an Aztec?* Franklin Watts, 1995.

"The Mesoamericans." Map. The National Geographic Society, 1997.

Mexico: A Story of Courage and Conquest. Videotape. History Channel, 1999. Four 50-minute tapes.

Milford, Susan. *Mexico!* Williamson, 1999.

Moon, Bernice and Cliff. *Mexico is My Country*. Cavendish, 1993.

Mora, Pat. *Uno, Dos, Tres = One, Two, Three*. Clarion Books, 1996.

Moran, Tom. *A Family in Mexico*. Lerner, 1987.

Morrison, Marion. *Mexico and Central America*. Franklin Watts, 1995.

Sayer, Chloe. *Arts and Crafts of Mexico*. Chronicle Books, 1990.

Seton, Ernest T. "The Onion Seller." *The Gospel of the Redman*. Seton Village, 1966.

"Spain in the Americas." Map. National Geographic Society, 1992.

Thomson, Ruth. *Aztecs: Facts, Things to Make, Activities*. Franklin Watts, 1992.

"Traveler's Map of Mexico." Map. National Geographic Society, 1994.

Winter, Jeanette. *Josefina*. Harcourt Brace, 1998.

Wood, Tim. *The Aztecs*. Viking, 1992.

The Geography of Mexico

Map Projects

Maps are excellent projects to display around the classroom. Three-dimensional maps bring to life the actual physical characteristics of an area. These map projects will help your students visualize the country of Mexico and its topography.

Here are two map-making projects which you may choose to use in your classroom.

Use the outline map of Mexico on page 14. Project the map onto a large sheet of white paper on a wall for the students to trace. After the outlines of the country and states are traced, have the students label the names of the states and their capitals. Students may want to color the states in the manner of a political map. Use the labels on the next page for this activity.

Have the students make a topographical map using the following recipe of flour, salt and water to make a dough mixture. Project the geographical regions map from page 17 onto a large piece of cardboard. Use the dough mixture to form the shape of Mexico, its mountains, and its plains. This map may take some time to dry properly. Have the students paint the various geographical areas in different colors. Small flags can be glued to toothpicks and stuck into the map to show important cities and places of interest.

Ingredients

- salt
- flour
- water
- food coloring
- newspaper or sheet of plastic to protect work surface

Directions

1. Mix one part flour with one part salt.

2. Stir in water until the mixture is thick but not too wet. The mixture should be the consistency of clay and should be able to be molded into mountains. You may add food coloring to the mixture at this point.

3. Allow this type of map sufficient time to dry; it may take one or two days depending upon the humidity.

4. You may paint the map after it is dry.

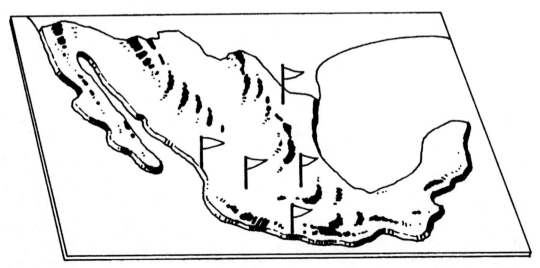

The United States of Mexico

Los Estados Unidos Mexicanos

Background Information

The Mexican Constitution, passed on February 5, 1916, declared the United States of Mexico to be a republic consisting of 31 states and the Distrito Federal (Federal District). The Distrito Federal is similar to Washington, D.C., in that the only city at this location is the national capital, Mexico City, referred to as Mexico, D.F.

As you can see from the chart below, Mexico City is one of the largest cities in the world. The metropolitan area of the city contains several more millions of people, making its total population around 19,000,000.

State	Population	Capital/Major Cities
Aguascalientes	800,000	Aguascalientes, Jesus Maria
Baja California Norte	2,000,000	Mexicali, Tijuana, Ensenada
Baja California Sur	500,000	La Paz, Cabo San Lucas
Campeche	600,000	Campeche, Escarcega
Chiapas	3,500,000	Tuxtla Gutierrez, Tapachula
Chihuahua	2,700,000	Chihuahua, Ciudad Juarez
Coahuila	2,100,000	Saltillo, Torreon
Colima	500,000	Colima, Manzanillo
Distrito Federal	10,537,000	Mexico City
Durango	1,350,200	Durango, Gomez Palacio
Guanajuato	3,980,200	Guanajuato, Leon
Guerrero	2,700,100	Chilpancingo, Acapulco
Hidalgo	1,900,400	Pachuca, Tula
Jalisco	5,800,000	Guadalajara, Puerto Vallarta
Mexico	10,915,900	Toluca, Texcoco, Tepotzotlan

The United States of Mexico *(cont.)*

Background Information *(cont.)*

State	Population	Capital/Major Cities
Michoacan	3,548,200	Morelia, Uruapan, Patzcuaro
Morelos	1,359,400	Cuernavaca, Cuautla, Tepoztlan
Nayarit	846,100	Tepic, San Blas
Nuevo Leon	3,098,700	Monterrey, Cerralvo
Oaxaca	3,021,500	Oaxaca, Huatulco
Puebla	4,326,100	Puebla, Tehuacan, Cholula
Querétaro	1,151,200	Querétaro, San Juan del Rio
Quintana Roo	593,600	Chetumal, Cancun, Cozumel
San Luis Potosi	2,002,000	San Luis Potosi, Valles, Matehuala
Sinaloa	2,310,800	Culiacán, Mazatlan, Los Mochis
Sonora	1,899,200	Hermosillo, Nogales
Tabasco	1,501,200	Villahermosa, Teapa
Tamaulipas	2,444,200	Ciudad Victoria, Tampico
Tlaxcala	763,700	Tlaxcala, Cacaxtla
Veracruz	6,528,200	Jalapa, Veracruz, Cordoba
Yucatan	1,363,500	Mérida, Celestun, Progreso
Zacatecas	1,378,300	Zacatecas, Fresnillo

Your students may have heard of Chihuahua and Tabasco. Ask them why those names are familiar. The small Mexican dogs originated in the area of Chihuahua, and the famous hot chili sauce came from Tabasco.

Ask students if they can think of other things that are named for the area from which they come. Examples might be frankfurters from Frankfurt, Germany, or hamburgers from Hamburg, Germany.

The United States of Mexico *(cont.)*

State Search

You can make a large classroom map by tracing the outline map on page 14 onto a piece of clear overhead transparency paper and projecting the map onto a large sheet of white paper. Trace the projected map onto the white paper using a pencil. Students can then trace Mexico and its states using a black marker.

Duplicate the state labels, enlarging them on the copier. Cut them apart and give each student a label. Have the students locate their states on the map and then color them. Paste or tape the state name to the map in the correct position. Use the map on page 15 as an answer key for the first activity. You can add more challenge to the activity by having the students locate and name the capital city of each state.

Mexico Puzzle

Following the directions as in the first activity, create another map of Mexico or use the map previously created. Cut along the black lines to separate the states into "puzzle pieces." Next, copy the map on page 16 onto a large piece of white paper using the overhead projector. Students can use it as a base on which to piece together their Mexico puzzle. Post a copy of the answer key on page 15 in the room for

1a. Baja California Sur	1b. Baja California Norte	2. Sonora
3. Chihuahua	4. Sinaloa	5. Durango
6. Coahuila	7. Nuevo Leon	8. Zacatecas
9. San Luis Potosi	10. Tamaulipas	11. Nayarit
12. Aguascalientes	13. Jalisco	14. Guanajuato
15. Queretaro	16. Hidalgo	17. Colima
18. Michoacan	19. Mexico	20. Morelos
21. Tlaxcala	22. Puebla	23. Veracruz
24. Guerrero	25. Oaxaca	26. Chiapas
27. Tabasco	28. Campeche	29. Yucatan
30. Quintana Roo	31. Distrito Federal (Mexico City)	

Map of Mexico

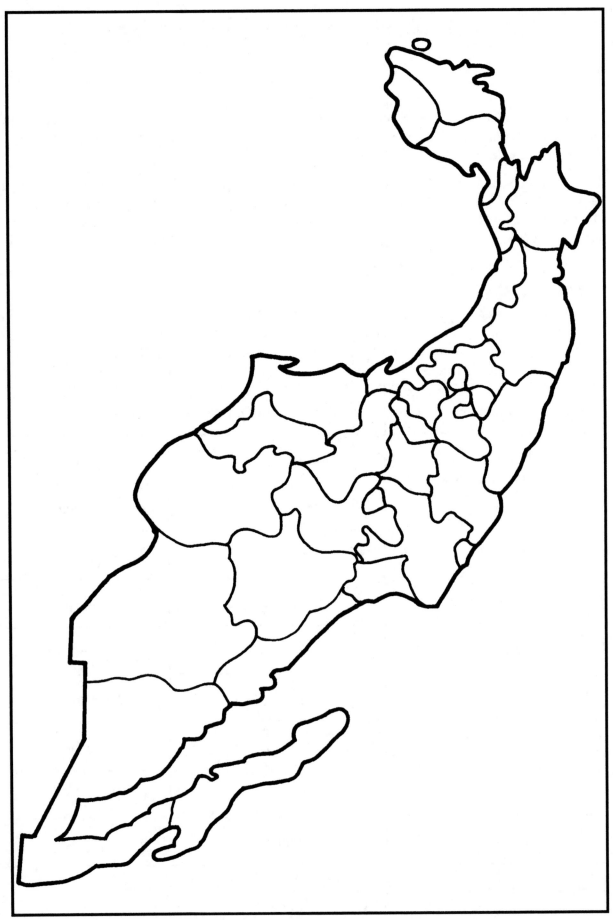

Map of Mexico Answer Key

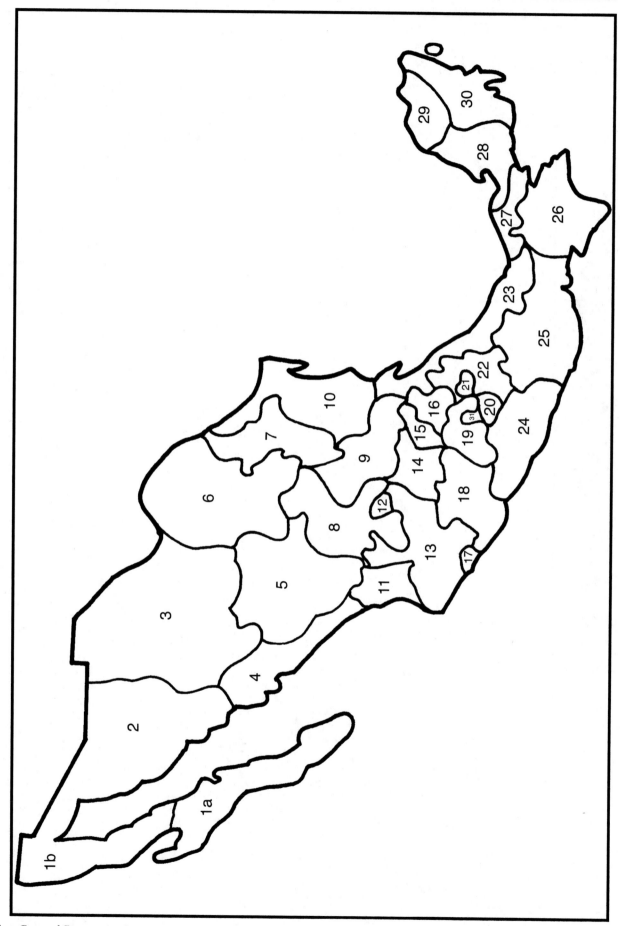

Outline Map of Mexico

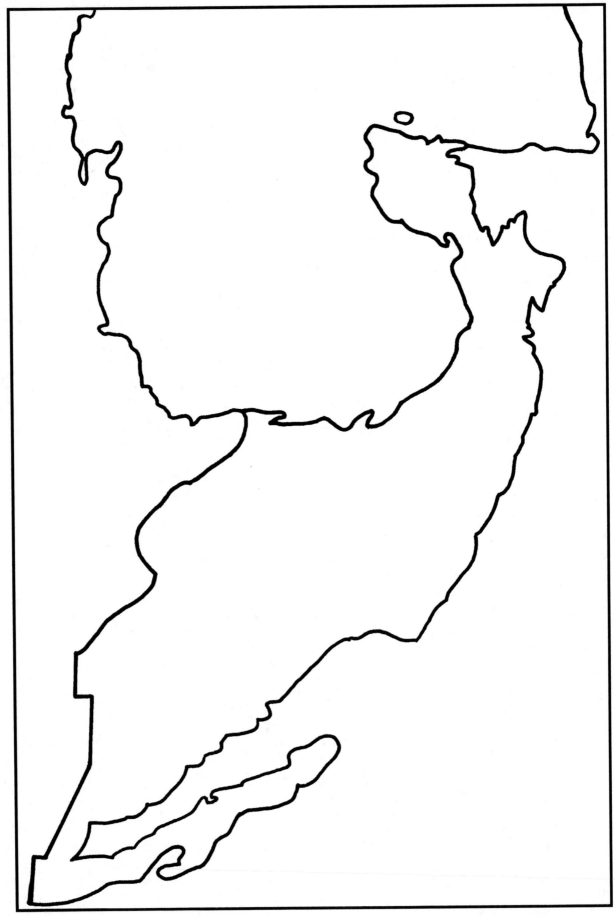

Geographical Regions of Mexico

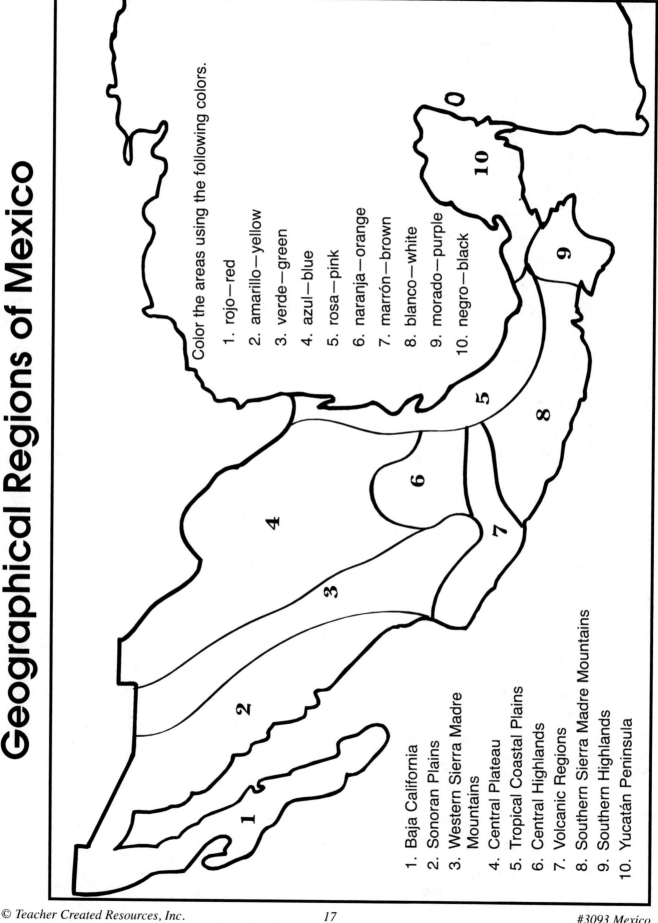

Color the areas using the following colors.

1. rojo—red
2. amarillo—yellow
3. verde—green
4. azul—blue
5. rosa—pink
6. naranja—orange
7. marrón—brown
8. blanco—white
9. morado—purple
10. negro—black

1. Baja California
2. Sonoran Plains
3. Western Sierra Madre Mountains
4. Central Plateau
5. Tropical Coastal Plains
6. Central Highlands
7. Volcanic Regions
8. Southern Sierra Madre Mountains
9. Southern Highlands
10. Yucatán Peninsula

United States of Mexico
Extension Activities

1. Which state has the same name as a small dog? _____

2. Look at Baja California Sur and Baja California Norte.

   What do you think Norte means in English? _____

   What do you think Sur means in English? _____

   Bonus: What do you think Baja might mean in English? _____

3. What is the name of the capital of the United States of Mexico? _____

   Distrito Federal (D.F.) means Federal District. The capital of the United States of America

   is Washington, D.C. What does D.C. mean? _____

4. Which Mexican state is the largest one? _____

5. Name the two smallest states (not D.F.). _____

   and _____

6. How many states share a border with the U.S.A.? _____

7. How many states are landlocked? _____

8. Which state is furthest north? _____

9. Which state is furthest south? _____

- -

Hint: Fold this section under before reproducing.

Answers: 1. Chihuahua 2. north, south Bonus: below or under 3. México, D. F. (Distrito
   Federal); D. C. means District of Columbia. 4. Chihuahua 5. Morelos, Tlaxcala

Which Way to Go?

Games for Learning Directions

In these games students will learn north and south directions. Assist students by pointing out on the map that Baja California has two sections, Baja Norte and Baja Sur. Explain to them that norte means north and sur means south. Have them point north in the classroom, and then have them point south.

For each student, make copies and cut out the norte and sur signs on page 20 and the este and oeste signs on page 21.

Game 1

Clear the room of desks, or play this game in an open area. This would make a good recess game on the playground. Designate the north side of the area and the south side of the area. Have the children line up in the middle of the area. When you hold up the norte sign, they should run to the north side of the area. When you hold up the sur sign, they should run to the south area. Have them return to the middle before you hold up a new sign.

If you do not have room for this game, you can have the students sit down for south and stand up for north. Hold the signs up very quickly, and you will have a room full of laughing children.

Game 2

Play the game as above, but play it like "Simon Says." If you want to do the game in Spanish, say, "Simon dice" (see-mon dee-say).

Game 3

Have a large map of Mexico in the room where everyone can see it. Divide the country into north and south with a line. Give each child a norte and sur sign, or give half the class norte signs and half the class sur signs. Point to places on the map and have the children hold up the appropriate signs. Repeat the game by dividing the map into east and west. Use the este and oeste signs from page 21.

Extension Activities

- Bring in compasses so the students can find the cardinal directions.

- Add east and west to the game.

- For more advanced groups add the intermediary directions NW, SW, NE, SE.

- Talk to the children about which direction they would have to go to reach certain points. Examples: the school cafeteria, home, the library, a friend's house.

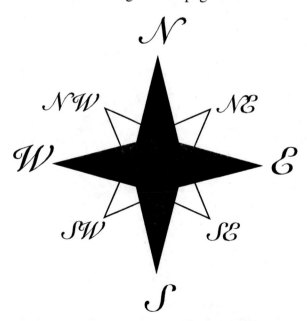

Which Way to Go? *(cont.)*

NORTE

SUR

20

Which Way to Go? *(cont.)*

ESTE

OESTE

Making a Bar Graph

A bar graph is a picture, which shows information. Bar graphs are used to help people understand numbers and statistics better. A bar graph compares things so you can see how they are alike or different.

In the bar graph on the next page, you are going to compare the populations of several states in Mexico.

Directions

1. Use a different color for each state.
2. Find the column for the first state, Aguascalientes.
3. See how many people live in Aguascalientes. Look on the left side of the graph to find that number.
4. Color the column above Aguascalientes from the bottom to the line with the number.
5. Do the same for each state, working across the graph.
6. When you are finished, you can compare the populations of these states.

Look at the bar graph that you have completed and answer the following questions.

1. Which state has the largest population? _____

2. Which state has the fewest people? _____

3. Which states have the same population? _____

4. Which states have a larger population than Baja California Sur, but a smaller population

   than Tlaxcala? _____

5. Name the three states on the list with the smallest populations.

   _____

6. How many more people live in Nayarit than in Campeche? _____

7. How many fewer people live in Baja California Sur than live in Tlaxcala?

   _____

8. Circle the one with the largest population.   Campeche   Tlaxcala   Nayarit

9. Circle the one with the smallest population.   Baja California Sur   Nayarit   Campeche

- -

Hint: Fold this section under before reproducing.

Answers: 1. Nayarit 2. Baja California Sur 3. Aguascalientes and Tlaxcala; Quintana Roo and Campeche 4. Quintana Roo, Campeche 5. Baja California Sur, Quintana Roo, and Campeche 6. 300,000 7. 300,000 8. Nayarit should be circled. 9. Baja California Sur should be circled.

Making a Bar Graph *(cont.)*

Use the information below to complete this bar graph. Remember to use a different color for each state. When you are finished, go back and answer the questions on page 22.

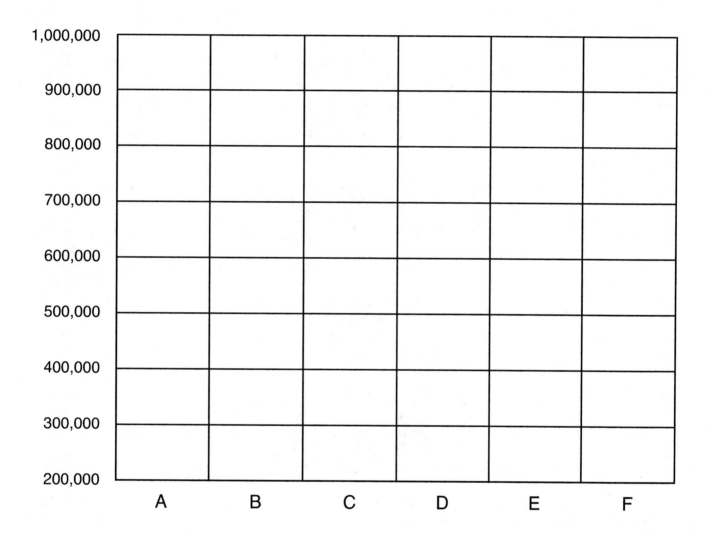

A. Aguascalientes 800,000

B. Nayarit 900,000

C. Quintana Roo 600,000

D. Baja California Sur 500,000

E. Campeche 600,000

F. Tlaxcala 800,000

The History of Mexico

The Aztecs and the Mayas

Background information

The Aztecs

The Aztec Indians were latecomers to Mexico. They came from the northwestern part of Mexico, or from what is now the southwestern section of the United States. Their legends are that they came from a place called Aztlán, the White Land, and it is from there that the name Aztec comes. They were also known as the Mexica, from which the modern name of Mexico comes. The Aztec culture came to its full power around A.D. 1300 and lasted until the Spanish conquest in 1521.

When the Aztecs arrived in central Mexico, the land was already divided among the many tribes that lived there; and there was not room for this new, nomadic group. But the Aztecs had a legend that had been handed down through generations. Many years before, a tribal elder had a vision. He had seen an eagle eating a snake while sitting on a cactus. The Aztecs believed that when they found that symbol they would be home. (See the flag legend on page 108.)

They saw the symbol on an island in the middle of Lake Texcoco. There they made their homes and began building their city. The city that they built was the great city of Tenochtitlán. The Aztecs drained much of the lake and built floating islands out of the silt. The islands are called *chiampas*. Their island city consisted of great pyramids, many houses, schools, and a great marketplace. It grew to be a city of 250,000 people, the largest city in the world at that time.

The Aztec influence spread throughout Mexico as they became powerful and feared leaders. The Aztecs adopted many of the traditions of older tribes such as the Maya. They had an accurate calendar, which was known as the Stone of the Fifth Sun. They used picture writing to make books called codexes where they recorded the history of their people and other important information. They also had a numbering and math system.

The Aztecs loved beautiful things. Art objects from all over central Mexico were imported to the great city of Tenochtitlán. The artisans made many beautiful bowls, masks, jewelry, and ornaments from gold, silver, obsidian, seashells, turquoise, and other precious metals and stones. The cloaks of some of the leaders were woven entirely from beautiful feathers of parrots, macaws, and the quetzal bird.

The common people of the villages lived in huts made of adobe bricks. Adobe is made from hardened mud. The houses had roofs of grass.

Coatl Serpent

Ehecatl Wind

Oceloti Jaguar

The Aztecs and the Mayas

Background Information (*cont.*)

The most famous emperor of the Aztecs was Moctezuma. He was the leader of the great nation when Cortés arrived from Spain. At first, he thought Cortés was the returning god, Quetzlcoatl; but he was deceived, and Cortés and his men overran the city and killed Moctezuma. The very last emperor was Cuauhtémoc. He was taken prisoner by Cortés and later killed. The traditions and the heritage of the Aztecs live on today. The country gets its name from this tribe, and many of its artworks remain. The large calendar stone of the Aztecs is a symbol of Mexico today and is seen reproduced everywhere. The vision of the Aztecs is the central picture on the Mexican flag. It is a picture of the eagle eating a snake while sitting on a cactus. It was the vision that brought the Aztecs to their home, and it is the symbol of Mexico today.

The Mayas

The Maya Indians were a much older culture than the Aztecs. They lived in the Yucátan Peninsula in the southeast section of Mexico. The Mayas built cities in the jungle areas, and they also had huge stepped pyramids and a powerful social system.

The Mayan empire was in the Yucatán Peninsula. Many of the old Mayan cities are still hidden away in the jungle that has overgrown them through the years. The Mayans were not the oldest civilization. The earlier Olmec people influenced much of their knowledge and culture.

The Mayas were the only people living in the Americas that had a complete writing system and were able to write in sentences. They used hieroglyphics that represented sounds. They were also great mathematicians and astronomers. Their highly complex calendar wheels helped them keep an accurate counting of the days of the year.

The Mayas were farmers and grew many native crops including corn, beans, squash, avocados, sweet potatoes, bananas, chilies, and watermelons. They used bows and arrows to hunt animals such as deer, turkey, ducks, pigs, and fish. They had mostly a vegetarian diet.

The Mayan culture began around 1500 B.C. and by A.D. 200 they had great cities and an extensive empire. The population may have been about 2,000,000 at its peak. The culture died out around A.D. 900. Today Mayan Indians still live in the area and practice many of the traditions of the great Mayans of old.

The ancient cities of the Maya are archaeological sites, and there are new ones uncovered each year.

Map of the Aztec and Mayan Empires

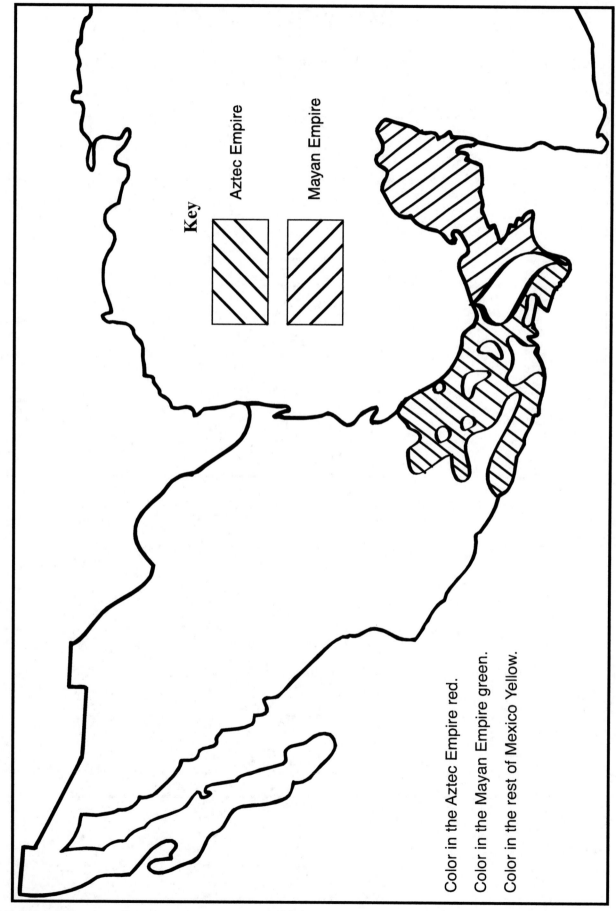

Key

Aztec Empire

Mayan Empire

Color in the Aztec Empire red.

Color in the Mayan Empire green.

Color in the rest of Mexico Yellow.

Mayan Math

The Mayan Indians used symbols for their numbers.

Here is how they wrote the numbers 0–19.

0	• 1	•• 2	••• 3	•••• 4
— 5	• — 6	•• — 7	••• — 8	•••• — 9
= 10	• = 11	•• = 12	••• = 13	•••• = 14
≡ 15	• ≡ 16	•• ≡ 17	••• ≡ 18	•••• ≡ 19

How do you think the Mayans wrote 20? _____

Answer the following arithmetic problems using the Mayan numbers.

1) 3 + 3 = _____

2) 16 – 5 = _____

3) 14 + 5 = _____

4) 2 x 6 = _____

Answer the following arithmetic problems using our numbers.

5) ••• + •• = _____

6) ___ + • = _____

7) ••• – •• = _____

8) ••• x •••• = _____

- -

Hint: Fold this section under before reproducing.

Answers:

20 ≡   1) • / —   2) • / =   3) •••• / ≡   4) •• / —   5) 10   6) 11   7) 1   8) 12

Model Aztec House

Directions

1. Students may want to color the houses brown or reddish brown to look like adobe brick.

2. Cut out the house pattern.

3. Fold down along the fold lines.

4. Glue the tab to the inside of the side wall where shown.

5. Have student cut out the roof on the next page. Fold and use tape to attach it to the house.

6. Students can make a village using these houses. Put the houses on a dirt surface and add small baskets of vegetables, small fire pits, and little animals.

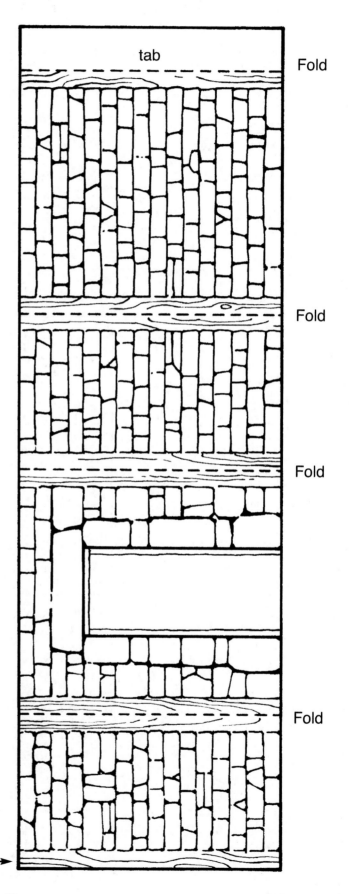

tab

Fold

Fold

Fold

Fold

Glue the tab to the inside edge of this wall. ——▶

Model Aztec House *(cont.)*

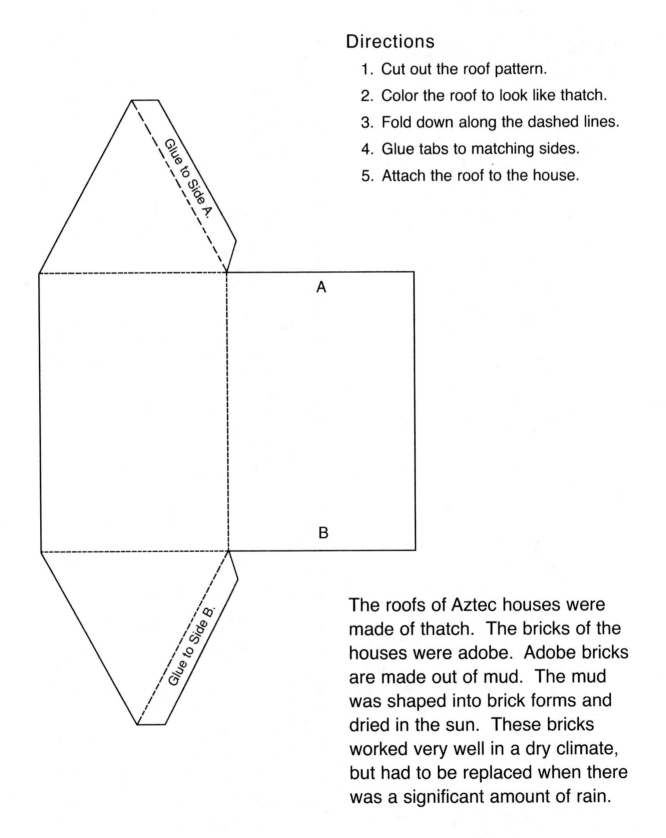

Directions

1. Cut out the roof pattern.
2. Color the roof to look like thatch.
3. Fold down along the dashed lines.
4. Glue tabs to matching sides.
5. Attach the roof to the house.

The roofs of Aztec houses were made of thatch. The bricks of the houses were adobe. Adobe bricks are made out of mud. The mud was shaped into brick forms and dried in the sun. These bricks worked very well in a dry climate, but had to be replaced when there was a significant amount of rain.

Mesoamerican Pyramids

The pyramids built by the Indians of Mexico are called step pyramids. These pyramids are built in tiers that look like large steps. People did not enter most of these pyramids. The pyramids were the bases for temples, which were built at the very top. Use the patterns on the following pages to build your own step pyramid.

Directions

1. If you want to decorate the pyramids, color them before assembling. Find pictures of the Aztec or Mayan pyramids to give you an idea of how to color them. The Indians used brightly colored paints on their pyramids.

2. Cut out the patterns on the following pages. Make sure to cut on the solid lines and fold on the dashed lines.

3. Tape or glue the overlapping edges of the boxes to hold them in place.

4. Insert the tabs into the slots of the boxes in this order:

   • First make the temple. Then attach the temple to Box 1, inserting the tabs into the slots and taping the tabs underneath where they won't show.

   • Next attach Box 1 to Box 2 and tape the tabs underneath.

   • Then attach Box 2 to Box 3 and tape it in place.

   • Fold the stairs on the outside dashed line. Fold the tabs back and tape them to the side of the pyramid at the opening of the temple.

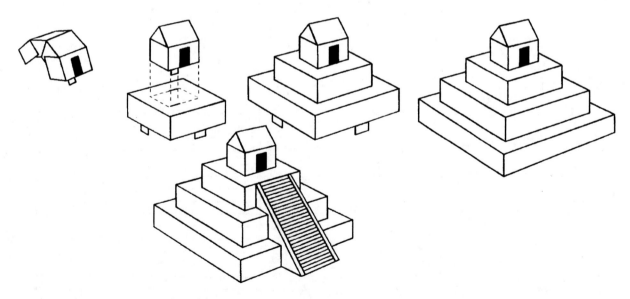

5. You can use your pyramid with the Aztec house to make a little village scene. You can make several pyramids to build a city. Look at some examples of ancient Mexican cities to give you ideas.

6. Making pyramids out of heavy paper or poster board will make stronger pyramids. You can also coat your pyramid with a thin layer of glue and sprinkle it with sand to make it look like it is made of stone.

Mesoamerican Pyramids *(cont.)*

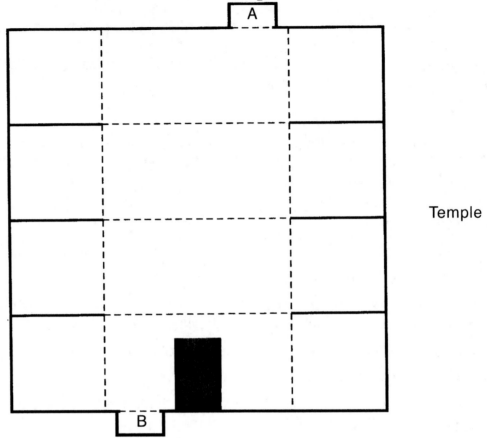

Temple

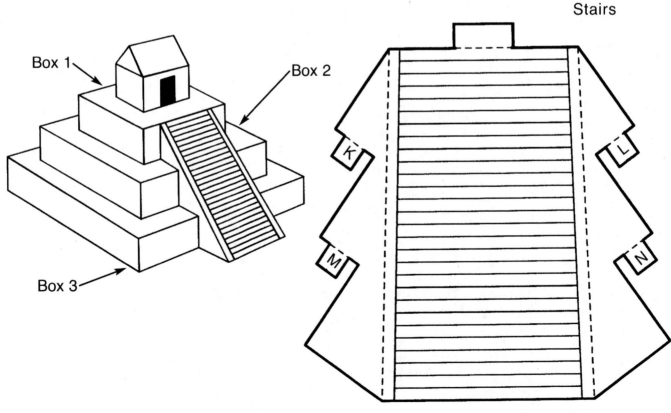

Stairs

Box 1

Box 2

Box 3

Mesoamerican Pyramids *(cont.)*

Box 1

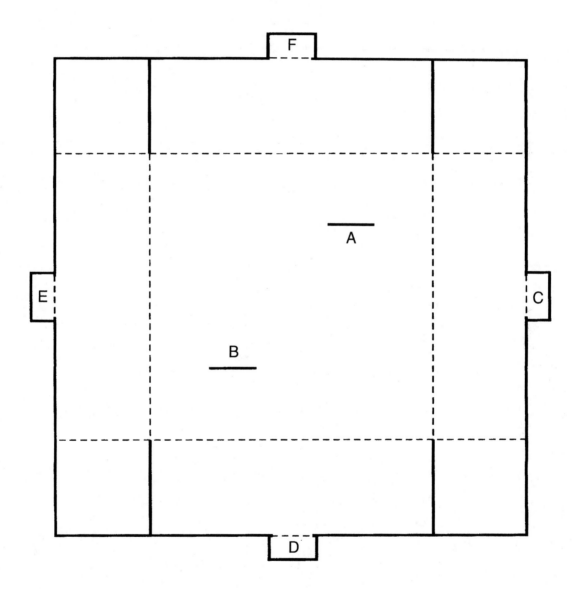

Mesoamerican Pyramids *(cont.)*

Box 2

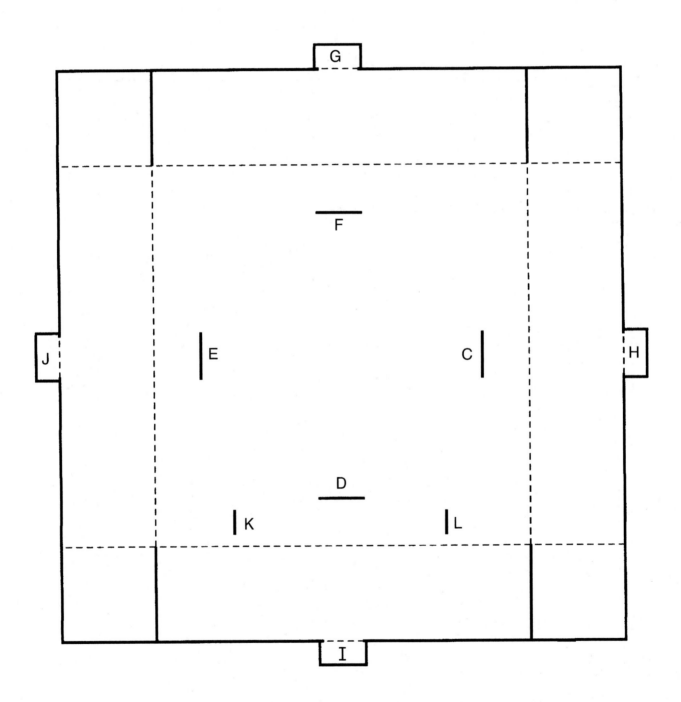

Mesoamerican Pyramids *(cont.)*

Box 3

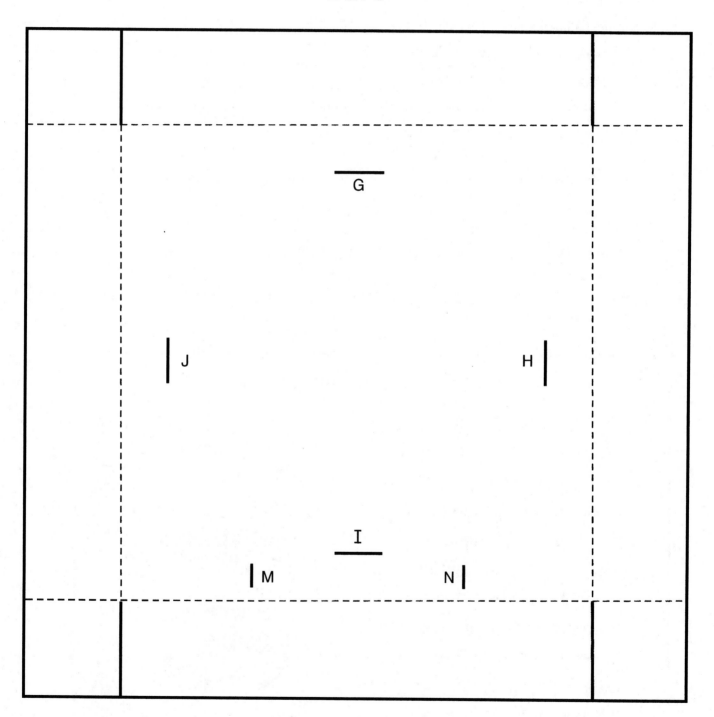

Teamwork Puzzle

This activity gives students the opportunity to discover how teamwork can be used for problem solving and critical thinking skills.

Directions

1. Duplicate the picture on page 37.

2. Cut the duplicated picture into quarters.

3. Copy each quarter at 200% larger.

4. Cut each duplicated quarter into quarters and duplicate each piece again at 200% larger.

5. Hand out the sixteen pieces to the class or team. Have the students color the pieces any way they would like.

6. Have students reassemble the 16 pieces into a large, colorful mural to display for the rest of the school.

Variations

1. You may choose to show students the picture before they attempt to solve it, or you may keep the finished picture a surprise.

2. You can duplicate the 16 pieces and keep dividing and enlarging to make a larger and more complicated finished project.

Background Information

The Colossal Head is an Olmec relic discovered near San Lorenzo at the archeological site of La Venta in Tabasco. The head is 9 feet (2.7 m) tall and weighs over 20 tons (18 metric tons). It was probably created during the early to middle Pre-Classic period about 1000 B.C. It is now at the Villahermosa Open-air Museum.

Teamwork Puzzle *(cont.)*

Important Dates in Mexican History

Mexico has a long history full of struggle and change. This is a brief list of major historical landmarks. Any of these events would be a topic for a research project.

10,000 B.C.	Human settlements are established in the Valley of Mexico.
1400 B.C. – 400 B.C.	Olmec civilizations are dominant in the east. They are the first great pre-Columbian civilization.
600 B.C.–1519 A.D.	Zapotecas are established in the Oaxacan area. They build the great city of Monte Albán.
500 B.C.–1519 A.D.	The Mayan civilization rises and falls in the Yucatan Peninsula.
200 B.C.	The building of Teotihuacán begins and continues in stages until about 700 A.D.
1345 A.D.	The Aztecs begins the building of Tenochtitlán, the city that later became Mexico City. The Aztecs flourishes as the dominant civilization in central Mexico until the Conquest.
1519	Hernando Cortés lands on the shores of Mexico and the Spanish Conquest of the Indians begins.
1521	Cortés captures Tenochtitlán and begins, the building of Mexico City.
1522–1821	Mexico is ruled by Spain.
1531	Juan Diego sees the vision of the Virgin of Guadalupe and she becomes an important symbol to Mexicans, even to this day.
1551	The first university in the Americas is built in Mexico City.

During the Colonial Period, life is very hard for the Mexican Indian people. They are forced to work on the large haciendas and in the silver mines. They are virtually slaves to the Spanish population.

September 15, 1810	The call for independence "Grito de Dolores" marks the beginning of Mexico's War of Independence from Spain. The cry was given by Miguel Hidalgo.

Important Dates in Mexican History *(cont.)*

1810–1821	The War of Independence takes place. The war ended in September, 1821.
1824	Mexico adopts its first Constitution. The first president is Guadalupe Victoria.
1846–1848	Mexico declares war on the United States over the issue of the Texas territory.
1863–1867	The French invade Mexico and Mexico falls under French rule. Maximillian becomes the emperor of Mexico, but he is executed three years later.
1867	The first Indian president, Benito Juarez, is elected after the fall of the French emperor.
1876 –1911	Porfirio Diaz is president of Mexico. This time period is known as the Porfiriato and is remembered for being a time of great wealth for the minority and great poverty for the majority.
1910 –1921	The Mexican Revolution. The struggles against the wealthy upper class lead to this eleven-year struggle for land and liberty. Famous names from this period include Pancho Villa and Emiliano Zapata.
1917	The New Constitution is signed.
1929 –2000	The Partido Revolucionario Institucional (PRI) becomes the dominant political party in Mexico and is not defeated in a presidential election until 2000.
1968	Mexico hosts the summer Olympics, and the first subway line in Mexico City begins operation.
1985	A huge earthquake hits Mexico City and kills thousands.
1994	NAFTA (North American Free Trade Agreement) takes effect, making the United States, Mexico and Canada one of the world's largest trading zones.
2000	Vicente Fox is elected president of Mexico. His election is the first defeat of a PRI candidate since 1929. He is a member of the PAN party.

Making a Time Line

Time lines are used to show when things happened in history. A time line shows the order of events in chronological order. That means in the order that they happened. For example, if you were going to make a time line of your life, it might look like this:

My Life Time line

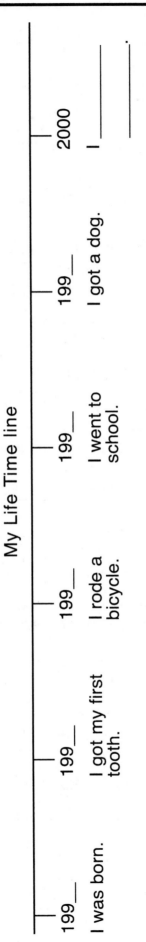

199__	199__	199__	199__	199__	2000	
I was born.	I got my first tooth.	I rode a bicycle.	I went to school.	I got a dog.		

Time lines can be used for any historical event.

Try making your own life time line below. Draw in the vertical lines and the dates that you need. Write events that have occurred in your life.

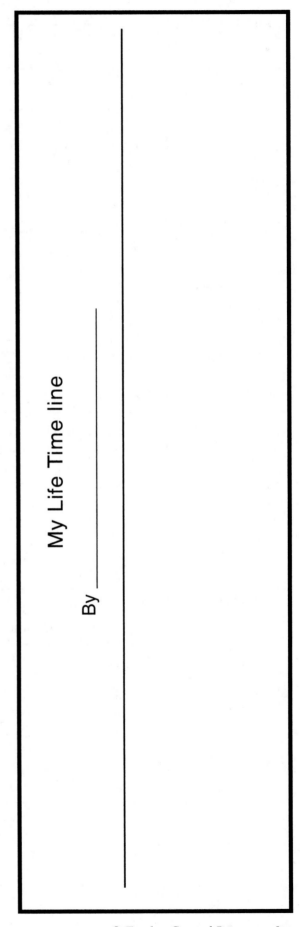

My Life Time line

By _____

40

Time Line Game

On the following pages are the parts to a Mexican history time line game. Explain to your students what a time line is and have them complete their personal time lines. After they have finished their time lines, have them discuss why they chose the events that they did for their time lines. Have them display their time lines. They might want to make larger ones on long sheets of paper.

Explain to the class that the Time Line Game is also a time line, even though it is not straight. It presents key events in the history of Mexico.

The game is a simple board game. Prepare a game board for each group of 4–6 players. Use buttons or beans for markers. Copy pages 43–46. Cut the game board sections along the dashed lines. Attach the sections, matching the tabs, and glue them to a large piece of construction paper. Encourage students to color and decorate their game boards and then laminate them for future use.

Each student spins the spinner. The one with the highest number starts. Then go clockwise around the group. The students take turns spinning, moving, and following the directions on the board. The first student to reach the end wins. To make the end more challenging, you may require that the winner has to have the exact number he or she needs to reach the last space.

The purpose of the game is for students to learn some of the major events in Mexican history. Each student should be given a chance to finish the game even after the first player reaches the end.

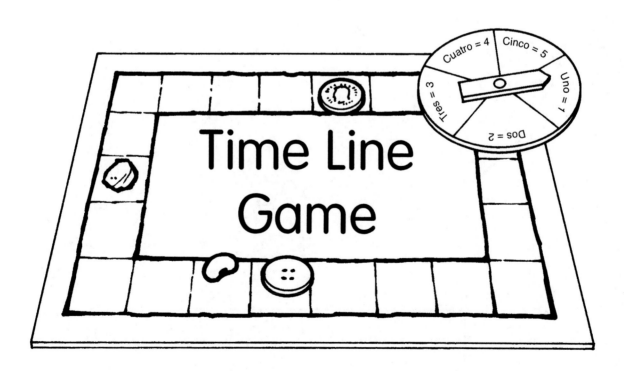

Time Line Game *(cont.)*

Copy the spinner circle and arrow below and glue the spinner to lightweight cardboard. Cut out the circle and the arrow. Punch a hole in the center of the circle and at the indicated spot on the arrow. Color the spinner with bright colors, but let the numbers show. Attach the arrow to the spinner with a brass paper fastener.

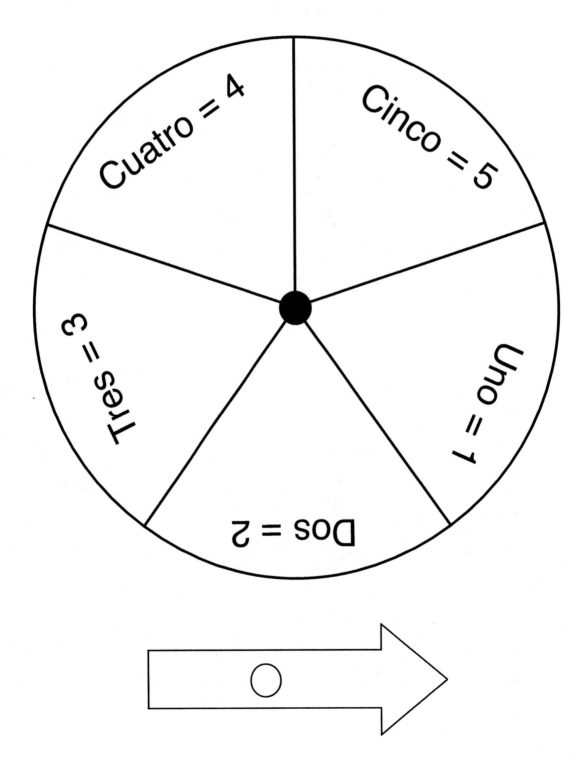

Time Line Game *(cont.)*

B

1519 A.D.

You see
Hernando Cortés
land on
Mexico's shores.

Directions:

- Cut this time line section

  along the dashed lines.

  Attached it to another

  game section by matching

  the tabs.

- Glue the four sections to a

  large piece of construction

  paper.

1350 A.D.
You help build
Tenochtitlan – the
capital of Mexico.

1300–1521 A.D.
You become a
Mayan Warrior.
Stand up and cheer!

500 B.C.–1450 A.D.

You fall off the
pyramid of the Sun
at Teotihuacan.

Lose a turn.

1200 B.C.–400 B.C.

You start here!

A

600 B.C.–1512 A.D.

You carve the great
Olmec Head.

Move ahead
3 spaces.

200 B.C.–750 A.D.

You help build the
great city of
Monte Alban.

Time Line Game *(cont.)*

1600 A.D. You own a hacienda— a large farm.	**Free space**	**1551 A.D.** You are the first student at the first university in the Americas. Stand up and bow.

C

Directions:

- Cut this time line section along the dashed lines. Attached it to another game section by matching the tabs.

- Glue the four sections to a large piece of construction paper.

1531 A.D.

Juan Diego sees the Virgin of Guadalupe.

Move ahead 3 spaces.

1522–1821 A.D.

Mexico is ruled by Spain.

1522 A.D.

You help to begin building Mexico City.
Pat yourself on the back.

1521 A.D.

You see Cortés capture Tenochtitlan.

Move back 1 space.

B

Time Line Game *(cont.)*

1810–1821 A.D.

You fight
in the
War of Independence.

Move ahead 2 spaces.

September 15, 1810 A.D.

You hear the
call for
Independence.

Cheer loudly!

1650 A.D.

You work in a
silver mine—it's
very hard work.

Lose a turn.

C

1824 A.D.

Mexico's
first constitution.

Move ahead 1 space.

1824 A.D.

The first President of
Mexico was
Guadalupe Victoria.

Who was our first
president?

1848 A.D.

The war with the United
States ends and you
are there when the
treaty is signed.

Move ahead 1 space.

D

Directions:

• Cut this time line section

along the dashed lines.

Attached it to another

game section by matching

the tabs.

• Glue the four sections to a

large piece of construction

paper.

Time Line Game *(cont.)*

D

1863–1867

French rule Mexico
5 years.

Lose a turn.

1867

The first Indian
president,
Benito Juarez,
takes office.

1917

You watch the
signing of the
New Constitution.

Directions:

• Cut this time line section

along the dashed lines.

Attached it to another

game section by matching

the tabs.

• Glue the four sections to a

large piece of construction

paper.

1968

Mexico hosts
the Summer
Olympic Games.

Name your
favorite sport.

1992

You sign the
NAFTA
agreement to
increase trade
for Mexico.

2000

You help elect
a new president–
Vincente Fox.

Now you've won!
It's fiesta time!

A

Mexico Information Search

Divide the class into teams of four or five students. Give each group an information search list. Discuss with the students the types of references they might use to find the answers. Allow them time to explore the library to find the resources that will give them answers to the questions they are assigned. Have students present their answers to the class. The groups can look for answers to all of the questions, or they can be assigned only certain questions to answer. Some of these questions are highly challenging for young students.

Group One (Grupo Uno)

1. Where is the Basilica of the Virgin of Guadalupe located?
2. What city in Mexico is most noted for the production of silver?
3. What section of Mexico was considered home to the Maya Indians?
4. In what year did Cortés invade Mexico?
5. Find a definition for *mariachi* and explain why it is important to Mexicans.
6. Who is currently the president of Mexico?

Group Two (Grupo Dos)

1. Where is Tulum located?
2. Which parts of Mexico are mostly desert?
3. Name the capital of the Aztec empire. What city is located there today?
4. During what years was the Mexican War of Independence fought?
5. For how long a term is the President of Mexico elected?
6. What is the story behind the Mexican coat of arms?

Group Three (Grupo Tres)

1. What river separates the United States from Mexico? Locate it on the map.
2. Name three metals that are mined in Mexico.
3. What was the name of the last great leader of the Aztecs?
4. Who were the boy heroes honored by the monument in Chapultepec Park?
5. How many states make up the country of Mexico?
6. Name the three artists who are considered the founders of modern art in Mexico.

Group Four (Grupo Cuatro)

1. What is the name of the long mountain range on the western edge of Mexico?
2. Name the five largest cities in Mexico.
3. What Indian group was responsible for the building of Monte Albán?
4. When was the Mexican-American War?
5. What are the colors on the Mexican flag, and what does each color represent?
6. What is the most popular spectator sport in Mexico?

Mexico Information Search *(cont.)*

Group Five (Grupo Cinco)

1. What is the name of the large volcano in the central plateau?

2. What is the basic monetary unit for Mexico? Find the current exchange rate.

3. What is the real name for the Aztec Calendar Stone?

4. In what year did Mexico City host the Summer Olympics?

5. What is the official language of Mexico?

6. What does *Grito de Dolores* mean? Who said it? When and why?

Group Six (Grupo Seis)

1. What is the name of the long mountain range on the eastern edge of Mexico?

2. What does the term *mestizo* mean?

3. What Indian group is thought to be responsible for building Palenque?

4. What battle of the Mexican-American War took place in San Antonio, Texas? In what year?

5. What is the legal voting age in Mexico?

6. What is the name of the largest park in Mexico City?

Group Seven (Grupo Siete)

1. What are the capital cities of these states: Sonora, Durango, Coahuila, Nuevo Leon?

2. What three crops from Mexico were new to the explorers from Europe?

3. Teotihuacan is an archeological site near Mexico City. It is famous for two very large pyramids. Name those two pyramids.

4. In what year did Benito Juarez become President?

5. Who was Quetzalcoatl?

6. What Mexican female artist was married to Diego Rivera?

Group Eight (Grupo Ocho)

1. What are the capital cities of these states: San Luis Potosi, Tamaulipas, Nayarit, Aguascalientes?

2. How many people live in Mexico City?

3. When was the Olmec culture at its height?

4. In what year did Pancho Villa die?

5. In what year was the Constitution of Mexico written?

6. What is the most common religion in Mexico?

Answers to Information Search

Group One

1. Mexico, D.F. (Mexico City)

2. Taxco

3. Yucatan Peninsula

4. 1519

5. *Mariachis* are wandering musical groups usually consisting of violins, guitars, trumpets, and a singer. They play lively folk music and often dress in *ranchero* costumes.

6. Vincente Fox was elected in 2000.

Group Two

1. Quintana Roo, on the eastern coast of the Yucatán Peninsula

2. Northern central, and the Baja

3. Tenochtitlan, now Mexico City

4. 1810-1821

5. six years

6. Before they settled in Mexico, the Aztecs had a legend that they were to travel until they found an eagle devouring a serpent while perched on a cactus. They saw that occur and settled where Mexico City is today.

Group Three

1. Rio Grande

2. copper, lead, silver, iron ore, gold (any three)

3. Moctezuma

4. Six military students who jumped to their deaths rather than surrender to the U.S. troops in 1846. The monument is called *Monumento a los Ninos Heroes*.

5. 31 states and 1 federal district (Mexico City, Districto Federal)

6. Jose Clemente Orozco, Diego Rivera, David Alfaro Siqueiros

Group Four

1. Sierra Madre Occidental

2. Mexico City, Guadalajara, Netzahualcoyotl, Monterrey, Puebla

3. Zapotecs

4. 1846-1848

5. green—independence; white—religion; red—union

6. soccer

Answers to Information Search *(cont.)*

Group Five

1. Popocatepetl
2. Peso (rate varies daily; check the Internet)
3. Stone of the Fifth Sun
4. 1968
5. Spanish
6. Cry of Dolores, Miguel Hidalgo (y Costilla), the cry to rebel against the Spanish, September 15, 1810

Group Six

1. Sierra Madre Oriental
2. people of mixed white and Indian ancestry
3. Mayan Indians
4. The Alamo in 1836
5. 18 years old
6. Chapultepec Park

Group Seven

1. Hermosillo, Durango, Saltillo, Monterrey
2. maize, tomatoes, tobacco
3. Pyramid of the Sun, Pyramid of the Moon
4. 1867
5. Quetzalcoatl was the Aztec god-king
6. Frida Kahlo

Group Eight

1. San Luis Potosi, Ciudad Victoria, Tepic, Aguascalientes
2. 10,500,000 (1992)
3. 1200-400 B.C.
4. 1923
5. 1917
6. Roman Catholic

Language and Literature

The Old Onion Seller

Preparation

Show the children pictures of Mexican markets.

Talk about Mexico City. Find it on the map. Tell the children that Mexico City is the Distrito Federal and is the capital of Mexico.

In a shady corner of the great market at Mexico City was an old Indian named Pota-lamo. He had twenty strings of onions hanging in front of him.

An American from Chicago came up and said, "How much for a string of onions?"

"Ten pesos," said Pota-lamo.

"How much for two strings?"

"Twenty pesos," was the reply.

"How much for three strings?"

"Thirty pesos," was the answer.

"Not much reduction in that," said the American. "Would you take twenty-five pesos?"

"No," said the Indian.

"How much for your whole twenty strings?" said the American.

"I would not sell you my twenty strings," replied the Indian.

"Why not?" asked the American. "Aren't you here to sell your onions?"

"No," replied the Indian. "I am here to live my life. I love this market place. I love the crowd and the red serapes. I love the sunlight and the waving palmettos. I love to have Pedro and Luis come by and say, 'Buenos días,' and talk about the babies and the crops. I love to see my friends. That is my life. For that I sit here all day and sell my twenty strings of onions. But if I sell all my onions to one customer, then my day is ended. I have lost my life that I love—and that I will not do."

52

The Old Onion Seller *(cont.)*

Discussion Questions

Have the students discuss why Pota-lamo loved the market. Reinforce the idea that the market is a colorful, social place. Buying and selling there are just as important socially as they are economically.

1. What were the things Poto-lamo looked forward to at the market?

2. How was Pota-lamo's life different from yours?

   Discuss how not having television, radio, or computers would affect his life.

   Where else would he get news?

3. Explain to the students that a serape is a blanket. People in Mexico wear serapes over their shoulders. Serapes are woven in bright colors.

   Have students talk about other things in the market that would have bright colors. (Clothing, food [chilies, oranges, pineapples], hair ribbons, etc.)

4. Do you think other people in the market might feel the same way that Poto-lamo did? Do you think the man from Chicago agreed with him? Do you think the man from Chicago would be happy selling onions all day? Why or why not?

5. Would you be happy sitting in the market all day selling something? What would you like to sell? Why?

6. Is there something you like to do that other people might think is a little silly?

7. Do you think it is important for everyone to like to do the same things? Why or why not?

Use the discussion questions to help the students understand the following two ideas from the story.

- Not everyone has to like doing the same things. It is important to have diversity in life.

- Sometimes we might think that a person acts one way for a reason, but the real reason may be something else. One might assume that the Indian sold onions to make money, but through the story we learn there is a more powerful reason that we might not be able to see immediately.

On the following page there is a picture of the onion seller. Let the students use this picture as a coloring page, or as a cover for a report about Mexico.

The Old Onion Seller *(cont.)*

Words You Know

Think you don't know any Spanish? Think again. Many of the words that we use in English were really Spanish words in the beginning.   Below are words with which you are probably already familiar. Did you know? They're Spanish!

patio	taco	poncho	plaza
rodeo	Canyon	chili	adobe

Even though these words came originally from Spanish, they have become common words in English. Use the words above in the sentences below to demonstrate your knowledge of their meanings.

1. My cousin's new house is made of _____ . It looks like dried mud on the outside.

2. John really enjoys the _____ . He likes to see the horses, the bull riders, and the clowns.

3. My family enjoys sitting on the _____ outside of our house. It is pleasant there in the evening.

4. I was glad when we went to the Mexican restaurant the other day. I was really hungry for a _____ .

5. When the rain came, my mother made me wear my _____ to stay dry.

6. I couldn't eat the _____ because it was too hot. It had a lot of peppers in it.

7. I really enjoyed seeing the Grand _____ . It was a marvelous sight.

8. When we strolled around the _____, we saw many other people enjoying the evening air.

- -

Hint: Fold this section under before reproducing.
Answers: 1. adobe   2. rodeo   3. patio   4. taco   5. poncho   6. chili   7. Canyon   8.

Spanish Word Face Mobile

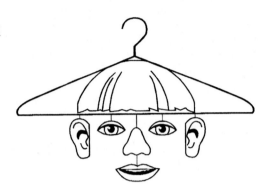

Materials

- brightly colored construction paper or poster board
- hanger
- hole punch
- pencil
- scissors
- string
- yarn

Directions

1. Using brightly colored paper, trace the designs from the next page onto poster board or construction paper and cut them out.

2. Choosing from the word list below, write the Spanish word for the matching body part on one side of the paper. On the other side, write the English word for that same part.

3. Fold down the tabs over the hanger and tape them to the back of the hair to secure it to the hanger. Punch a hole in the top of the ears, eyes, mouth, and nose. Then hang each with string from a coat hanger to make a cheerful face that will help you learn the Spanish words.

4. You can add color to the mobile by covering the hanger with yarn.

Word List

ear—oreja	hair—pelo	mouth—boca
eye—ojo	head—cabeza	nose—nariz

Extension Activity

Play "Simon Says" in Spanish.

1. "Simon says" is *Simón dice* (see-moan´ dee´-say) in Spanish.

2. "Touch" is *toca* (toe´-ka) in Spanish

3. The names of the body parts require articles.

la cabeza (ka-bay´-sa)	*el ojo* (oh´-ho)	*el pelo* (pay´-low)
la nariz (nar-eez´)	*la boca* (bo´-ka)	*la oreja* (o-ray´-ha)

4. An example of the game might be:

Simón dice toca la cabeza.	The children touch their heads.
Simon dice toca el ojo.	The children touch their eyes.
Simon dice toca la nariz.	The children touch their noses.
Toca la oreja.	The children should not touch anything, because you did not say "Simon dice."

Spanish Word Face Mobile *(cont.)*

Pattern

Spanish Count to Ten Book

Use the following directions to help students fold the counting book pattern on page 59 or to make their own book. To prepare the counting book, first duplicate (page 59) and cut along the outside solid lines.

Directions

1. Fold the page in half lengthwise and crease. (The words should be on the outside.)

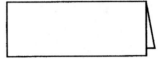

2. Fold in half widthwise, then fold again. Unfold completely. The paper will have eight sections.

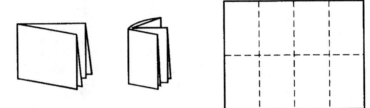

3. Refold along the center fold widthwise. Have fold at top of paper. Cut along the vertical fold (solid side on page 59) sto the next horizontal fold halfway down. Unfold.

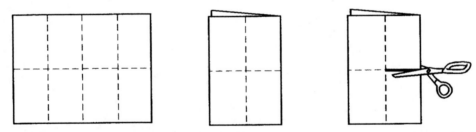

4. Refold lengthwise. Push the ends together so that the center bows out on either side. Fold the pages so that they all go in the same direction to make the pages of the book.

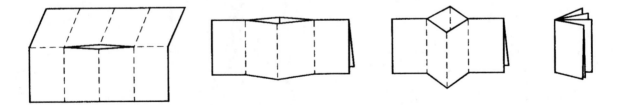

Suggested Activities

1. Have students color the book and add pictures to the pages.

2. You may want to have the students make their books of plain paper and write the numbers on the pages along with their own pictures.

3. Have students practice counting things in the room using Spanish numbers.

4. Use the books to complete page 60.

Spanish Count to Ten Book *(cont.)*

diez = 10

nueve = 9

Count to Ten in Spanish

uno = 1
dos = 2

siete = 7
ocho = 8

tres = 3
cuatro = 4

cinco = 5
seis = 6

Can You Do Spanish Math?

Solve the word problems below. Write the answers in Spanish.

1. If Miguel has **diez** apples and Pilar takes **dos**, how many apples will Miguel have left?

   _____

2. Juanita is **ocho** years old. Her brother is **dos** years older. How old is her brother?

   _____

3. **Tres** children are waiting for the bus. **Cinco** more come to join them. How many are now waiting for the bus? _____

4. **Uno** boy is in the classroom. **Nueve** students join him. How many are in the room?

   _____

5. **Diez** puppies are in the window. **Siete** are sold in one day. How many puppies are still in the window? _____

6. **Diez** tacos are on the plate. Alicia eats **seis** tacos. How many tacos are left?

   _____

7. Maria told the teacher that **tres** times **tres** equals _____.

8. Juan knows that **dos** times **tres** equals _____.

9. Carlos has **diez** cookies to share with **cinco** friends. How many will each friend get?

   _____

10. If **cuatro** children read **dos** books each, how many books will they read?

    _____

- -

Hint: Fold this section under before reproducing.

Answers:	1. ocho	2. diez	3. ocho	4. diez	5. tres
	6. cuatro	7. nueve	8. seis	9. dos	10. ocho

60

My Book of Spanish Words

On the following pages, you can make a little book about Mexico and learn some Spanish words at the same time.

Directions

1. Cut out the pages.

2. Color the pictures on each page.

3. Arrange the pages in alphabetical order.

4. Staple the pages together and add a bright cover.

5. Learn to pronounce your words and teach them to your family and friends.

- -

Mexico From A to Z

Come and Learn Some Spanish with me!

Name _____

Nombre

- -

My Book of Spanish Words *(cont.)*

A a ____

A is for **aguacate.**

(a-gwa-ka-tay)

Aguacate is Spanish for avocado. This is a fruit that is popular in Mexican cooking.

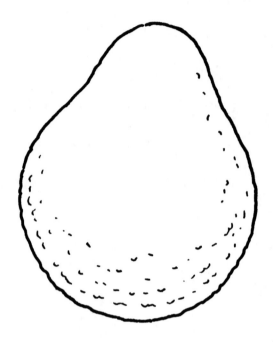

B b ____

B is for **burro.**

(boo-ro)

Burros are used to help farmers get to the market.

Burros are useful in the mountains.

My Book of Spanish Words *(cont.)*

C c _____

C is for **chile**

(chee-lee)

A chile is a very popular
Mexican pepper. They make
the food tasty and spicy hot!

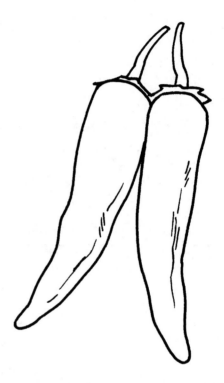

D d _____

D is for **dos.**

(doughs)

Dos is the number two.

My Book of Spanish Words *(cont.)*

E e _____

E is for **enero.**

(ay-nay-ro)

Enero is January. In Mexico,
it only snows in the mountains.

F f _____

F is for **fiesta.**

(fee-ay-sta)

A fiesta is a party. Everyone
looks forward to fiestas in
Mexico.

My Book of Spanish Words *(cont.)*

G g _____

G is for **girasol.**

(he-row-sole)

A girasol is a sunflower. Sunflowers grow in many parts of Mexico. The flowers are beautiful, and the seeds are yummy!

H h _____

H is for **huevos.**

(hway-vose)

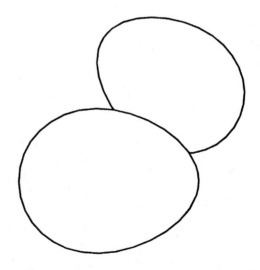

Huevos are eggs. They are also called batidos.

My Book of Spanish Words *(cont.)*

I i

I is for **iguana.**

(ee-gwa-na)

Iguanas are large green lizards.
They are very common in the
Mexican deserts.

J j

J is for **Juan Diego**

(hwan dee-ay-go)

Juan Diego is a famous person
in Mexican history. He was the
man who saw the Virgin of
Guadalupe.

My Book of Spanish Words *(cont.)*

K k ‾‾‾‾

K is for **kilómetro.**

(kee-lo-may-tro)

A kilómetro is a measure of distance. Road signs in Mexico have kilómetros instead of miles.

L l ‾‾‾‾

L is for **lima.**

(lee-ma)

A lima is a lime. Lime is a popular flavor in Mexico and is added to many foods.

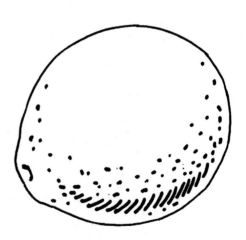

My Book of Spanish Words *(cont.)*

M m _____

M is for **mariposa.**

(ma-ree-po-sa)

A mariposa is a butterfly.
Mexico is famous for its
beautiful Monarch butterflies.

N n _____

N is for **nariz.**

(na-rees)

Nariz is a nose.

My Book of Spanish Words *(cont.)*

O o _____

O is for **ojo.**

(o-ho)

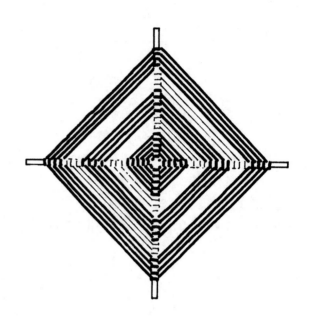

Ojo is an eye. Ojo de Dios is a God's Eye made of strings and sticks.

P p _____

P is for **poncho.**

(pon-cho)

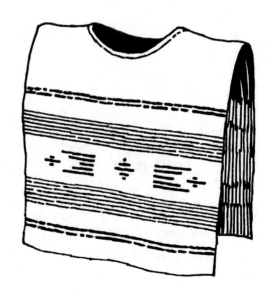

A poncho is a cloak that is slipped over the head. Ponchos are often made in bright colors.

My Book of Spanish Words *(cont.)*

Q q _____

Q is for **queso.**

(kay-so)

Queso is cheese. Many
Mexican dishes contain cheese.

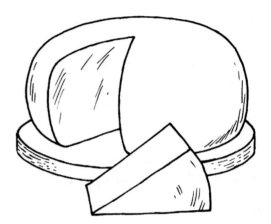

R r _____

R is for **rana.**

(rah-nah)

A rana is a frog. You can hear
frogs singing in the tropics of
Mexico.

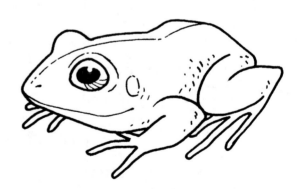

70

My Book of Spanish Words *(cont.)*

S s

S is for **sandía.**

(san-dee-a)

Sandía means watermelon. In Mexico watermelon is a cool treat on a hot day.

T t

T is for **taco.**

(ta-koe)

Tacos are one of the favorite foods in Mexico and they are popular in the United States, too.

My Book of Spanish Words *(cont.)*

U u

U is for **uno.**

(oo-no)

Uno is the number one.

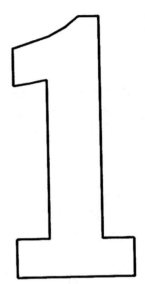

V v

V is for **vainilla.**

(bay-een-ee-ya)

Vainilla is the flavoring that you taste in vanilla ice cream. Did you know that it is a plant?

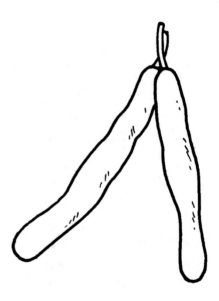

72

My Book of Spanish Words *(cont.)*

W w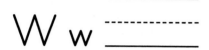

W is for W.C.

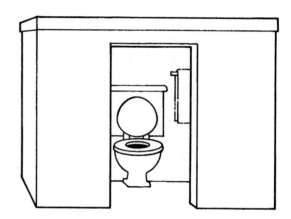

A W.C. is a water closet. That is what bathrooms are called in Mexico and in some other countries.

X x

X is for **xilófono.**

(zee-low-foe-no)

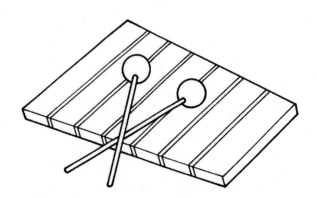

A xilófono is a musical instrument. In English, we call it a xylophone. It is a popular instrument in Mexico, along with a marimba, which is similar.

My Book of Spanish Words *(cont.)*

Y y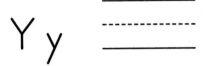

Y is for **yema.**

(yay-ma)

Yema means egg yolk. It is the yellow center of a huevo.

Z z

Z is for **zócalo.**

(zoe-koe-lo)

A zócalo is an area where people can gather to meet, talk, and walk. Most Mexican towns have a zócalo in the center with trees, benches, and a bandstand.

The
Wildlife
and
Environment

A New World Full of Gifts

When the Spanish came to the New World in 1519, they were looking for gold. But many of the treasures they found were just as valuable and often surprising.

Can you imagine a life without tomatoes, peanuts, or turkeys? What about never having chocolate or corn? All of these things are native to the Americas, and the people of Europe were surprised to find them here.

When they first found potatoes, the Europeans did not think they were fit to eat! But when they learned that they could feed more people from a field of potatoes than a field of grain, they learned to like them.

Explorers also found chilies and pineapples. Sunflowers were growing on the great plain and becoming a valuable source of oil. The cotton growing in the new world was much better and stronger than anything that had been used in Europe before.

The Aztecs were the last people to settle in the Valley of Mexico, high on the volcanic mountains of central Mexico. The explorers found that the Aztecs were skilled doctors and healers. The Indians used natural remedies found in the plants of Mexico. Many of the Spanish conquistadors preferred the medicine of the Aztecs to the doctors in Spain at that time. The Aztecs also practiced surgery with obsidian knives. Obsidian is a stone, but the knives were as sharp as modern steel instruments.

The Mexicans received many new animals from the Spanish. There were no horses in the New World before the conquistadors came. The Indians were amazed at the men on horseback. The conquistadors also introduced donkeys and oxen. Pigs, Spanish chickens, cattle, and sheep were other animals brought to the Americas from Europe.

Oats, wheat, rye, and barley were introduced to the New World by the explorers and settlers. These crops flourished in the climates of temperate regions. Sugar grew successfully in the tropical areas. After its introduction, coffee became an important cash crop in the New World.

Not everything that the explorers brought was good. The disease of smallpox came from Europe and killed many of the Indians because they were not immune to the disease.

Discussion Questions

1. How would your life be different without tomatoes, chocolate, or potatoes?

2. Discuss the good and bad things that the explorers brought to the Americas.

3. Invent a new plant that you would like to discover. What would it look like? Would you be able to eat it? Would it have some other use? Draw a picture of your plant.

A New World Full of Gifts *(cont.)*

Extension Activities

- Have students brainstorm about the many uses for corn. Write the list on a large sheet of paper. The paper can even be cut into the shape of an ear of corn or a kernel of corn. Add to the list throughout the unit as students come up with new uses.

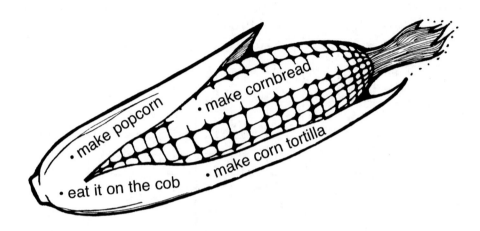

- Have students brainstorm about the importance of the turkey.

- Have a student or team of students research corn and the turkey and write a report to read to the class.

- Listed below are some products that were given to the world by Mexico.

tomatoes	pumpkins	chilies
vanilla	avocados	coconuts

- Have students bring in examples of these products. They can bring in the actual items or pictures of them. Have them tell the class about the product. Ask the class to share ideas about how we use these plants and add them to the list.

- Discuss other food items that were discovered in the New World. Some of them are:

pineapple	peanuts
potatoes	sunflowers

- Extra research projects can also be assigned to students who want to report on these New World plants.

Teamwork Activity

Have students sit in teams. Give each team a piece of paper and a pencil. At the top of the paper write the name of one of the plants listed above. Have the teams pass around the paper to each team member. Each student can then write a use for the item at the top of the paper.

Have students brainstorm about what life would be like without these plants today. What would they miss? What would be better about life? What would be worse?

Gifts from the New World Puzzle

Puzzle

Use the words in the box to complete the crossword puzzle.

avocado	peanuts	sunflowers
chili	pineapple	tomato
coconut	potato	vanilla
cotton	pumpkin	

Across

1. circus food
4. spikey covered fruit
7. a hot taste
8. a green fruit

Down

1. mashed or baked _____
2. reach for the sun
3. an ice cream flavor
4. a Halloween favorite
5. white and flaky
6. a red fruit
7. a clothing fabric

Gifts from the New World *(cont.)*

Riddles

When the explorers came to the Americas, they found many new plants and animals there. Several important plants and animals came from Mexico.

Can you solve these riddles to discover what three of the plants and animals were? (Hint: Two are plants, and the other is an animal.) Write the answers in the boxes.

Riddle 1

My first is turn without an end;

My second opens locks, my friend.

On holidays I'm on a plate

The Pilgrims thought I tasted great!

What am I?

Riddle 2

I grow in the ground,

And sometimes I am ground.

I come in many colors

And grow taller than your head.

I love to go to cookouts,

And I often pop up at theaters.

What am I?

Riddle 3

I am good cold or hot.

In wintertime, I hit the spot.

People like me on ice cream.

In cakes and icing, I'm a dream.

I am something you can favor;

I may be your favorite flavor.

What am I?

Gifts from the New World *(cont.)*

Answer Key

Page 78

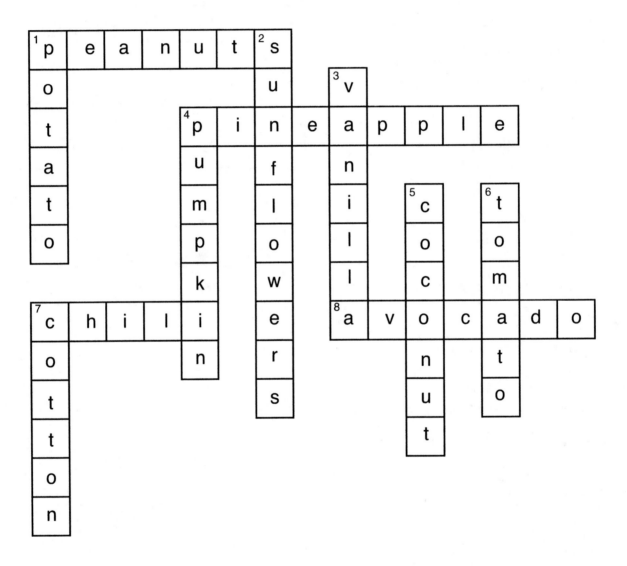

Page 79

Riddle 1—turkey   Riddle 2—corn   Riddle 3—chocolate

Climate and Vegetation

Mexico has many different climates. In Mexico, you will find deserts, rain forests, tropical ocean climates, and grasslands. Much of Mexico is higher than 5,000 feet (8,000 km) above sea level. This means that even though the Tropic of Cancer cuts across Mexico, the mountains keep the central plateau from being as hot as other tropical areas. Low-lying areas of the south are warm and tropical, but the land dries out further north where there are deserts.

The lowlands in the eastern coast of Mexico are tropical. This part of the country has lush vegetation and evergreen tropical forests. Bamboo, mangrove, swamp cypresses, and other swamp plants grow here. Between July and October, the Yucatán Peninsula and the southern part of Mexico are occasionally affected by the hurricanes from the Gulf of Mexico or the Caribbean.

The lowlands on the southern Pacific coast of Mexico are warm and tropical also. Most of the rainfall is in the summer, and the temperatures all year long are warm. Breezes from the ocean make this area very pleasant for tourists. The plants in this area tend to be brush land with scrubby grasses, and low bushes and shrubs.

The northwest region of Mexico is mostly desert. This part of Mexico includes Baja California, Sonora, and Sinoloa. There are areas of farming here in the oasis where cotton, wheat, rice, sugar cane, fruits, and vegetables are grown. The desert land here supports little vegetation, which consists mainly of various types of cactus.

Two long mountain ranges extend down both the Pacific coast and the Gulf coast of Mexico. The western mountain range is called the Sierra Madre Occidental and the eastern range is called the Sierra Madre Oriental. Between these two ranges of mountains is the Central Plateau. This plateau is where most of the people in Mexico live. Due to the higher elevation, the Central Plateau is cooler and drier than the tropics. This is the area of Mexico where there are many farms and ranches.

The weather in the southern Central Plateau has wet summers and moderate temperatures. The northern section of the plateau has wet summers, steppe climate, sub-tropical semi-desert, and desert climate. The vegetation of the plateau varies widely with the seasons. Scrubland becomes lush grassland with the summer rains. The plateau supports many varieties of cactus, mesquite, yucca, and agave. There are coniferous and deciduous woodlands on the mountains around the plateau. The types of trees growing on the slopes of the mountains include evergreen and deciduous oaks, arbor-vitae, juniper, pines, and other conifers.

Land Regions of Mexico

Choose a different color for each region and color in the box located next to that region. Then color the areas on the map with those same colors. (Remember that on any map blue is used for water only.)

desert

warm and sunny

savannas (tropical grasslands)

warm with dry winters

tropical rain forests

steppes (semi-arid grasslands)

Amazing Animals of Mexico

Read and discuss the following paragraphs with the students. Then, have them complete pages 84 and 85.

Beautiful butterflies, colorful birds, mischievous monkeys, and deadly snakes live on the varied landscapes of Mexico. The jaguar was a symbol of power to the Aztecs, and the colorful birds gave their feathers for the traditional costumes.

One of the great, mysterious attractions in Mexico is the migration of millions of Monarch butterflies to the eastern part of Michoacán. No one understands why the butterflies make this journey each year, but it is a beautiful sight as millions of orange and black wings flutter through the air.

Iguanas and Gila monsters are two of the lizards that live in the desert areas of Mexico. You can often see children selling iguanas by the roadsides in the country, but stay away from the Gila monsters because they are poisonous. Other desert animals include coyotes, lizards, prairie dogs, and rattlesnakes.

Spider monkeys and parrots like to live in the tropical forests where there is an abundance of trees. The spider monkey winds its way through the branches like a professional acrobat, and can sometimes be a pest if you are eating food nearby. The parrots have brightly colored feathers that make them easy to see in the green foliage. Macaws also live in the tropical forests. The quetzal bird has long, brightly colored feathers that the Aztecs used for their ceremonial costumes. Unfortunately, the quetzal is becoming very rare.

One peculiar animal that lives in the jungle areas is the peccary. This funny-looking animal is a type of wild hog, and is called a javelina in Spanish. Ringtail cats also enjoy the jungle areas for hunting. Other cats that live in the Mexican jungles are ocelots, jaguars, and margays.

The dolphin and starfish can be found in the ocean areas of Mexico. Dolphins like to play off the shore, diving and swimming in the clear waters of the Pacific. Gray whales are sometimes also sighted off the shores of Baja California. Many other sea fish live near the Mexican shores and make fishing a big industry for the country.

The interesting and varied animal life of Mexico is as fragile as life anywhere. Much of the wildlife is disappearing as the land is developed for logging, farming, and industry. A blight along the coast of the Caribbean has claimed many of the palm trees, which are a natural habitat for the parrots and macaws. Logging is changing the migration patterns of the butterflies. Ecology is very delicate, and we must all work to protect our planet and the animals that live here.

Suggested reading: *The Three Little Javelinas, The Hummingbird's Gift, The Tale of Rabbit and Coyote*. (See bibliography.)

Environments of Mexico

Mexico has many different natural environments. Talk about the animals below and decide where you think they would live. Think about what kinds of homes they would need and what kind of food they might eat.

Cut out the circles below and place the animals in the environment in which they live on

spider monkey

peccary

dolphin

butterfly

Gila monster

starfish

parrot

ringtail cat

rattlesnake

coyote

lizard

Environments of Mexico *(cont.)*

Desert

Tropical Forest and Jungle

Ocean

Bread Dough Animal Ornaments

Materials

- 3 slices of white bread per child
- 3 tbsp. (.45ml) white glue
- lemon juice
- acrylic paints
- brushes
- water
- yarn
- acrylic sealer spray

Directions

1. Remove bread crusts.

2. Tear bread into small pieces and place in a bowl. Add glue and lemon juice.

3. Mix together with fingers until the mixture has a smooth, dough-like texture.

4. Let the children form the dough into an animal, fish, insect, or bird that they have studied. (See Environments of Mexico).

5. Add a yarn loop into the dough if it is to be used as an ornament.

6. Let dry and paint as desired.

7. Spray with an acrylic sealer.

The dough can be made ahead and stored in a plastic bag. It can be kept in the refrigerator for several weeks.

Bark Paper Painting

Since before the time of Columbus, the Indian people of Mexico have been making paper. They make their paper from the bark of trees. They paint colorful pictures on the bark paper to record their way of life and important events in history. Before the Spanish conquest, the people painted pictures about their religious ceremonies showing their gods, priests, warriors, and predictions for the future. The paintings of today usually show everyday life such as weddings, fiestas, farming, or fishing.

Bark paper is often seen in the states of Puebla, Veracruz, and Hidalgo. It is called *amate*. Mulberry trees (moral) are used to make a whitish shade of paper, and the fig tree (xalama) makes a darker shade of paper.

The bark is peeled from trees by the men of the village. The women wash the bark and boil it in lime water in large pots. The bark is rinsed and laid on boards like large heaps of laundry. The wet pulp is then beaten with rocks and shaped into paper sheets and left to dry in the sun. The paper is then decorated with very colorful paints.

Materials

- brown grocery bags
- bright tempera paints
- water
- sponges
- brushes

Directions

1. Tear brown grocery bag into rectangles.

2. Crush the paper and then smooth it out.

3. Sponge brown tempera paint sparingly onto the paper to make it appear mottled. Rub off any extra and allow to dry.

4. The design on the following page is a typical folk art design that can be used for the bark painting.

Have students draw or trace simple folk art designs onto the paper and paint the designs with bright tempera paint. Brushes with sturdy nylon bristles for acrylic paints will work well.

Extension Activity

Students may want to try making their own paper. Put a cup of water into a blender and add facial tissues until you get a paste. Add red and green food coloring until the mixture turns brown. Pour the mixture onto a smooth surface to shape and dry. Use magic markers to draw pictures. This method makes thicker paper that the students can use to make hanging decorations.

Folk Art Design

Environments of Mexico

Color the picture below and identify the desert animals. Write or tell a short story about what you think is happening in this picture. Share your story with the other students in your class. Choose your favorite animal and find out more about it.

Legends and Traditions

Mexican Holidays

The people in Mexico love to have fiestas and celebrations.

There are many local customs and parties throughout the year. It is common in Mexico to see processions and fireworks. During these celebrations, people enjoy music and dancing, too.

Here is a list of some of the most important holidays celebrated in Mexico. Read about the holidays and see how many are similar to the holidays you celebrate in your home.

JANUARY

1   Año Nuevo (New Year's Day) is an official Mexican holiday.

6   Día de los Santos Reyes is the day when Mexicans exchange Christmas presents. This is in remembrance of the day that the wise men brought gifts to the baby Jesus. This is the last day of the Christmas season festivities.

17   Feast Day of de San Antonio de Abad is a religious holiday during which the Catholic Church allows animals to enter the church for blessing.

FEBRUARY

5   Día de la Constitución is an official holiday that commemorates the signing of Mexico's Constitution.

24   Flag Day is a national holiday for honoring the Mexican flag.

MARCH

5   Carnaval is an official Mexican holiday that kicks off a five-day celebration before Lent. Beginning the weekend before Lent, Carnaval is celebrated exuberantly with parades, floats and dancing in the streets. Port towns such as Ensenada, La Paz, Mazatlán, and Veracruz are excellent places to watch Carnaval festivities.

21   The Birthday of Benito Juárez, a famous Mexican president and national hero, is an official Mexican holiday.

APRIL

Semana Santa   Semana Santa is the holy week that ends the forty-day Lent period. This week includes Good Friday and Easter Sunday. It is Mexican custom to break confetti-filled eggs (cascarones) over the heads of friends and family for good luck.

Mexican Holidays *(cont.)*.

MAY

1   Primero de Mayo (May 1st) is the Mexican national holiday that is equivalent to the United States Labor Day.

5   Cinco de Mayo is the Mexican national holiday that honors the Mexican defeat of the French army at Puebla de los Angeles in 1862.

10   Mother's Day – Due to the importance of the mother in Mexican culture, Mother's Day is an especially significant holiday.

JUNE

1   Navy Day is an official Mexican holiday.

SEPTEMBER

1   Annual State of the Union – This date changes, but the President gives his annual address to the nation near the beginning of September.

8   Día de Nuestra Señora is a local holiday in the Baja that celebrates Baja's first mission.

16   Mexican Independence Day celebrates the day that Miguel Hidalgo delivered "El Grito de Dolores," a speech that called the Mexican people to fight for independence while announcing the Mexican revolt against Spanish rule.

OCTOBER

12   Día de la Raza – This day celebrates Columbus' arrival to the Americas and the historical origins of the Mexican race.

NOVEMBER

1, 2   Día de los Muertos is an important Mexican holiday that merges Pre-Columbian beliefs and modern Catholicism. Europe's All Saints' Day and the Aztec worship of the dead contribute to these two days that honor Mexico's dead. The festivities actually begin with the evening of October 31st.

20   Mexican Revolution Day is an official Mexican holiday, which celebrates the Mexican Revolution of 1910.

Mexican Holidays *(cont.)*

DECEMBER

12	Día de Nuestra Señora de Guadalupe (The Day of the Virgin of Guadalupe) is celebrated with a feast honoring Mexico's patron saint. This is Mexico's largest and most important holiday.
16	Las Posadas reenacts Joseph and Mary's search for shelter in Bethlehem with candlelight processions that end at various nativity scenes. Las Posadas continues through Christmas Eve.
24	Noche Buena (Christmas Eve) is an important day in the Christmas traditions. It is the last night of the Posada when Mary and Joseph end their search for a place to stay. There is usually a fiesta, with food and piñatas on this night after the church services.
25	Navidad – With the rest of the Christian world, Mexico celebrates Christmas day. It is a religious day in Mexico. Gifts are given on January 6th.

Fiesta!

In addition to the many festivals and fiestas listed on the holiday list, Mexicans also celebrate saint's days. Each town or village has its own patron saint, and the day of that saint's birthday is another reason to have a party.

Fiesta means "feast day" in Spanish, and food is a large part of the celebrations. Stands selling corn-on-the-cob, cotton candy, homemade potato chips, and tortillas line the streets where people gather to watch the festivities. The wonderful smells of food are everywhere.

A main part of the day is a procession through the streets. A band that plays traditional music accompanies the procession. The procession winds around through the streets, and everyone who is able takes part in the walk. Often statues of the saint will be carried by the people. Sometimes people in the parade will wear masks of animals like tigers or jaguars.

As soon as it gets dark enough, the fireworks begin. The fireworks are very dramatic and wonderful. They are often attached to large bamboo structures known as castillos. Castillo is Spanish for castle, and many of these structures are several stories high. When the fuse is lit, the fireworks climb the structures and turn large wheels that shoot sparks out into the night.

Some fireworks are attached to toritos, or little bulls. These are shaped like the heads of bulls and are worn by men and boys who chase after people in the crowd while the sparks are shooting from their heads! It is a scary spectacle as everyone runs from the fire, but even though it is dangerous, everyone laughs and enjoys the fun. Sometimes the fireworks will last long into the night as different men wear the toritos and chase the crowds. There will sometimes also be other shapes, such as baskets of flowers or monkeys.

By the time the fireworks have ended, it is usually very late. Everyone heads for home, happy from another fiesta day.

94

An Easter Tradition

Easter is a time of many fiestas and celebrations in Mexico. It is one of the happiest and most decorated holidays.

In the United States, we color Easter eggs and have an Easter egg hunt. In Mexico, they do something very different!

Mexican children make cascarones and hit their friends over the head with them!

It is the tradition to fill empty eggshells with colorful confetti, then to break the egg on the head of a friend. When the confetti showers down on them, they will be showered with good luck for the coming year.

You can make your own cascarones for a springtime celebration.

Materials

- eggs (save egg cartons)
- large needle
- bowl
- colored paper
- glue
- markers, crayons, or paint

Directions

1. Carefully wash and dry the eggs thoroughly before using. Use a large needle to put one hole in each end of an egg. Have an adult hold the egg over a bowl and blow into one end of it. The insides of the egg will come out of the other end and into the bowl.

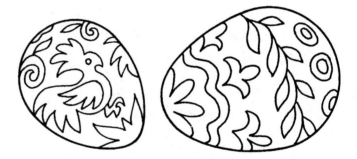

2. Rinse your eggshell, and let it sit in an egg carton or somewhere safe for a while to dry. If you want to dye your eggshell with cold-water dye, you should do it at this time.

3. While your egg is drying, cut little pieces of colored paper into confetti.

4. Gently fill your eggshell with the little confetti. You may have to make one of the holes in your egg a little larger. Be careful not to crack or break your egg. When it is full, glue a small piece of colored paper over the hole.

5. Decorate your eggs with markers, crayons, or paint. Now you are ready to have a fiesta with your cascarones! Remember, you are wishing your friends good luck, so be careful not to hurt them!

If you are going to have your fiesta outside, it is a good idea to fill your eggs with birdseed so that your bird friends can have a fiesta when you are finished!

The Posada Song

One of the most colorful traditions of Mexico is the Posada. It is a nine-day celebration that starts on December 16th and ends on Christmas Eve. In Mexico, people travel from house to house and perform the Posada every night during this time. After the Posada is performed, there is a party with a piñata for the children.

The Posada is a song that is like a short play. This song tells the story of how hard it was for Mary and Joseph to find a place to stay for the Baby Jesus to be born. To perform the Posada, your class should be divided into two groups.

The "Outside" (O) group represents Mary and Joseph. They are asking for a place to stay.

The "Inside" (I) group represents the people who have no rooms for the travelers. They keep turning Mary and Joseph away until the end when they realize how important the travelers are.

O: In the name of heaven, please let us in.
   My lovely wife cannot walk anymore.

I: This is not an inn. Get out of here.
   I cannot open up. You may be a thief.

O: Don't be cruel. Have mercy on us.
   Our Lord in heaven will reward you.

I: It's time for you to go and stop bothering us.
   Because if you make me angry, I will beat you up.

O: We are very tired coming from Nazareth.
   I am a carpenter. My name is Joseph.

I: I don't care what your name is. Let us go back to sleep.
   I have already told you that I am not going to open.

O: My dear sir, only for one night.
   The Queen of Heaven is asking for shelter.

I: Well, if she is a queen and needs a place to stay,
   Why is she walking alone so late at night?

O: My wife is Mary. She is the Queen of Heaven.
   And she is going to be the mother of the Son of God.

96

The Posada Song *(cont.)*

I: Is it you, Joseph? Your wife is Mary?
   Among other travelers I didn't recognize you.

O: May God reward you for your generosity.
   And may our Heavenly Father bless you with happiness.

I: Honored is this house! And the day that we welcome
   The pure and beautiful Blessed Virgin Mary.

On the last night of the Posada these verses are added. Everyone should say them together.

Come in blessed travelers,

Travelers make yourselves at home.

Even when the shelter is poor

It is offered with much love.

Oh, graced pilgrim,

Oh, most beautiful Mary.

I offer you my soul

So you may have lodging.

Humble travelers,

Jesus, Mary and Joseph,

I give my soul for them

And my heart as well.

Let us sing with joy

As we all remember

That Jesus, Mary and Joseph

Honor us by coming here.

A Mexican Christmas Tradition

The children in this picture are reenacting the Posada. They are asking for shelter in Bethlehem. The name for Bethlehem in Spanish is Belen. The other children are carrying candles called velas in Spanish.

Make Your Own Piñata!

A traditional shape for the piñata is the star. This shape is easy to make and fun to break at your party. Here is an easy way to make a piñata.

Materials

- a large round balloon
- strips of newspaper to cover the balloon
- whole newspaper
- flour paste

- masking tape
- string or twine
- colorful tissue paper

Directions

1. Make your flour paste by mixing ¼ cup (50 g) sugar and ¼ cup (50 g) flour with 1¼ cups (420 ml) of water. You may add oil of peppermint or wintergreen to make the mixture smell nice. Make sure you mix the ingredients thoroughly to avoid lumps.

2. Blow up the balloon and tie the end closed.

3. Dip the strips of newspaper in the paste and wipe off the excess.

4. Wrap the strips around the balloon, leaving a small hole at the balloon opening. Make sure that you let the paper dry between layers, and cover the balloon three or four times.

5. Let the entire coating of strips dry, and then prick the balloon and pull it out through the small hole.

6. Make five cones from sheets of newspaper and tape them to the ball in a star pattern.

7. Cover the entire piñata with a layer of paste and colorful tissue paper. You may want to fringe the tissue paper and add tassels to the ends of each star point.

8. Fill the piñata with candy or other goodies through the hole in the top, then close the hole with tape and cover with tissue paper.

9. Cut two small parallel lines in the piñata. Loop a piece of yarn through the opening to hang the piñata.

10. Suspend the piñata from a high point such as the ceiling or a basketball goal.

11. Use a broomstick to hit the piñata, but make sure the hitter is blindfolded first. Be careful that everyone stands out of the way of the hitter. Take turns allowing each child to strike at the piñata three times until the star breaks and everyone can rush for the prizes!

This activity is a good opportunity to teach good sportsmanship and sharing, as everyone should be allowed to have some of the candy when the piñata breaks.

Make Your Own Piñata! *(cont.)*

Sample of Completed Piñata

Instead of using candy, you can offer other gifts to your friends. Make, or purchase, inexpensive gifts. Tape a different number on each. Place the gifts in a covered box. Next, cut out squares of brightly-colored construction paper. Write a number on each so that the paper square numbers match the numbers on the gifts. Roll up each numbered square, wrap a rubber band around the paper, and place it in the piñata as you would the candy.

Have a Piñata Party!

Piñatas are an important part of any party in Mexico that includes children. At the end of the Posada or at birthday parties, piñatas provide excitement and pleasure for the children. These large, colorful shapes made of papier-mâché and bright paper decorations are filled with candy and treats for the children. The piñatas are hung up high and children take turns hitting the piñatas with sticks, hoping to break it open so that the prizes will fall out for everyone to claim. Younger children get some help from the adults, but older children are blindfolded as they try to strike the piñata.

Many of the piñatas in Mexico are as large as small children and have the shapes of animals, clowns, or favorite characters from stories. The main body of the piñatas may be made of clay or papier-mâché. The outsides are decorated with brightly-colored frilly paper.

The history of the piñata is long and unclear. It is thought that Marco Polo may have brought the idea from China. Other legends record it as a tradition that was already known in Mexico before the conquistadors. It was a well-known tradition in Europe in the sixteenth and seventeenth centuries.

You're Invited!

Please join our class for a piñata party!

Date: _____

Time: _____

Location: _____

We hope you can come join the fun!

Sincerely,

_____

(student name)

Cinco de Mayo

Cinco de Mayo (the fifth of May) is a Mexican national holiday also celebrated by Hispanics in the United States. Hispanic students and others enjoy this as a fiesta that comes near the end of the school year and celebrates their ethnic identity as Mexican-Americans and Spanish speakers.

How did it all start? During the American Civil War (1861-1865), while the United States was fighting internally over the slavery issue and economics, Europeans decided to invade Mexico to collect some bad debts. France also wanted an empire, so in 1862, they sent an army to take over Mexico.

Benito Juarez, the first president of Mexico (who was also a Zapotec Indian) resisted the French invasion, rallying the Mexican people to resist. The Battle of Pueblo took place on May 5, 1862. The Mexican Army, under General Ignacio Zaragoza, defeated the well-trained French Army with poor Indian peasants. The victory proved that the French were not invincible. The French "empire" in Mexico collapsed five years later when Emperor Maximilian was executed.

Along with the music and dances of Mexico that play a big part in any Cinco de Mayo celebration, the flag of Mexico is displayed. It consists of three wide vertical stripes as follows: red on the left, white in the middle, and green on the right. On the white stripe is an eagle on a cactus with a snake in its mouth. According to legend, the ancient Aztecs saw such an eagle and took it as a sign to build the capital city, Tenochtítlan, on that spot.

Color the Mexican flag below. Then, as a challenge, find a picture of Benito Juarez, Maximilian, or Ignacio Zaragoza in an encyclopedia or other reference book and draw his picture on the back of this paper.

The Virgin of Guadalupe

The image of the Virgin of Guadalupe is seen all over Mexico. Her picture appears in churches, on buildings, in Mexican homes, on people's clothing, on bookmarks, magnets, candles, calling cards, bumper stickers, and in many other places. Understanding the importance of this icon is an important part of teaching students about the cultural background of Mexico. The Virgin of Guadalupe is the patron saint of Mexico. Since most Mexicans are Catholic, it is impossible to study the culture of the country without including the story.

The Virgin of Guadalupe is an extremely important figure in the Mexican culture. The largest and most important fiesta in the Mexican year is the one that celebrates the appearance of the Virgin Mary, the mother of Jesus Christ, to a Native Mexican in 1531. The holiday is celebrated on December 12th with religious observances, processions, fireworks displays, and other festivities. Millions of people travel to the Basilica of Guadalupe in Mexico City to pay homage to the miracle.

The story of the appearance of the Virgin is told on page 104. The significance of the story lies in the fact that the appearance of the Virgin to a Native Mexican impressed upon the Indian people of Mexico that God was concerned not only for the Spanish conquistadors, but also for the Indian people. The Virgin of Guadalupe was their assurance that even though their old gods were destroyed by the Spanish conquerors, the Indians were accepted as part of the new religion that was introduced to their land by the Catholic priests. This acceptance allowed Mexico to become a Catholic nation, a fact that has strongly influenced the development of the country through the centuries.

Enjoying the Story

1. Read the story to the students. Have them discuss how they would feel if the appearance had happened to them. Have them give their reasons for the appearance of the picture on the tilma of Juan Diego.

2. Have the students describe what they think the Virgin of Guadalupe might have looked like. Let the students draw their own pictures, or do a group composite picture taking ideas from all of the class.

3. Let the students color the picture of the Virgin of Guadalupe. Bring in a color version of the picture and have the students compare their choice of colors to the traditional picture.

4. Hang the pictures around the room for the Mercado. In Mexico, you would see the picture everywhere.

The Virgin of Guadalupe *(cont.)*

The Story of the Appearance of the Virgin of Guadalupe

In early December in the year 1531, a native Mexican man was walking across a hill called Tepeyac. The man's name was Juan Diego. He was on his way to church. Suddenly all of the birds stopped singing. In front of Juan Diego, a beautiful woman appeared. She told Juan that she was the Mother of Jesus. She told Juan to go to the bishop and tell him that she wanted a church built on that hill.

Juan did as she asked, but the bishop did not believe the story Juan told.

Juan went back to the hill the next day. He told the lady that the bishop did not believe him. She told Juan to come back the next day, and she would give him proof.

Juan had a sick uncle. He was very worried about his Uncle Bernardino. The next day, Juan decided that he would get a priest to help his sick uncle. Instead of going to see the lady, Juan went around the other side of the hill, but the lady found him there. She told him again that he should go see the bishop. This time she would give him proof that she had appeared to him.

Juan went up on the hill. Even though it was winter and very cold outside, Juan found roses lying on the ground. He picked up the roses and put them in his cloak. The lady reached out and arranged the flowers. She told Juan to return to the bishop. She also told him not to worry about his Uncle Bernardino, because he was not sick anymore.

Juan took the roses in his cloak and went back to the bishop. The bishop was very surprised to see roses in the middle of winter. But the roses were only part of the surprise.

When Juan Diego dropped the roses out of his cloak, the bishop stared in surprise at the front of Juan's clothing. There on the front of his cloak was the image of the beautiful lady. It was a picture of her just as Juan Diego had seen her on the hill. No one could explain how the picture had appeared.

The cloak (called a tilma) of Juan Diego still has that picture on it. The tilma is in the Basilica of the Virgin of Guadalupe in Mexico City. The picture is over 450 years old and is still on the cloth. Millions of people travel to see the image every year.

The Virgin of Guadalupe *(cont.)*

Optional Activity

Traditionally, the components of the Virgin of Guadalupe icon have symbolic importance. Here is a brief summary which can be shared with the students. Reproduce the chart below and the illustration on page 106. Distribute copies and discuss the information with the class.

Eyes	Face	Hands
The eyes look down to show humility. She is not God, even though she is very important. Indian gods never looked down; they looked straight ahead.	Her face and hair are dark like the Indians. She has a gentle look of care and compassion. The Indians believed that the inner person was revealed by his or her face. Her femininity shows in her face.	Her hands are held in a prayerful manner. This is also the Indian manner of offering. She is offering something that is to come from her.
Maternity Bands	**Stars**	**Sun Rays**
The high band around her waist shows that she is expecting the birth of a child.	The Indians believed that stars and comets brought news of a new era. The stars on her mantle (not shown in illustration) indicate the beginning of a new age. The stars also indicate that the she is the Queen of Heaven.	The sun was an important symbol in the Indian religions. She is standing in front of the sun, but she does not extinguish it. The rays also signify holiness.
Mantle	**Moon**	**Angel**
The turquoise color was a color of significance to the Indians. It was a color reserved for their great god Omechihuatl. The blue indicates unity for everything that exists. Blue is also a symbol of eternity and human immortality.	She is standing on the moon (not shown in illustration) to indicate that she is greater than the god of the night, the moon god.	The angel is a messenger from God, giving a new message to the world. Mary is above the angels to indicate her position in heaven.

The Virgin of Guadalupe *(cont.)*

106

Miracles of the Milagros

When people make pilgrimages to the Shrine of the Virgin of Guadalupe in Mexico City, they have special requests to ask of Mary. Some bring flowers in her honor, some come slowly on their knees in prayer, and others purchase small offerings made of gold, silver, brass, or tin.

The metal offerings are called *milagros*. They represent many types of prayers that people make to the Virgin. For example, if someone has a problem with his or her foot, then the *milagro* is in the shape of a foot. If a farmer has a sick pig or any other sick animal, then one may find a *milagro* representing the sick animal for sale. Crops, houses, saints, farm implements, cars, boats, and people of all ages can also be found in the shapes of *milagros*.

The people take their *milagros* and pin them on a special board near the altar or, in some churches, on the robes of a saint. These tokens can also represent a thank you for a prayer that is answered.

Materials

- aluminum pie tins
- scissors
- pencil or fine-point permanent marker
- hole punch
- yarn

Directions

1. Begin by discussing something for which the students are thankful or something that worries them.

2. Have them draw their designs on the pie tins and simply cut them out. (Adult supervision and assistance is urged when working with younger children.)

3. After they are finished, punch a hole at the top of each *milagro* and tie yarn through the holes so that they can be displayed or shared with the class.

The Legend of the Mexican Flag

The Mexican flag dates back to 1821. It is divided into three vertical sections. The left section is solid green for independence. The center section is white for religious purity. The right section is red for national unity.

In the middle of the center section is the Mexican coat of arms. This symbol depicts an eagle perched on a cactus and devouring a snake. This symbol is borrowed from an Aztec legend. The Aztecs were latecomers to the central plateau of Mexico. When they arrived from the north around 1325, most of the land was already divided among the tribes who had already been living there. The Aztecs believed that their deity Huitzilopochtli had given them a vision: that when they saw an eagle devouring a snake while perched on a cactus, they would be home. They spotted this on an island in the middle of Lake Texcoco. It is here that they established their home of Tenochtitlan.

When the conquistadors arrived in 1519, Tenochtitlan was larger than the great cities of Europe. Today, as then, it is the largest city in the world.

Materials

- copies of flag (page 109) and coat of arms (page 110)
- rulers
- tape or glue
- crayons or markers
- scissors

Directions for Flag

1. Color the flag on page 109 according to the legend.

2. Cut the flag out and tape it to a ruler or dowel.

3. Wave your flag and cheer for Mexico.

Directions for Coat of Arms

1. Cut out the coat of arms on page 110.

2. Tape or glue it to a large piece of paper for a "Class Coat of Arms."

The Legend of the Mexican Flag *(cont.)*

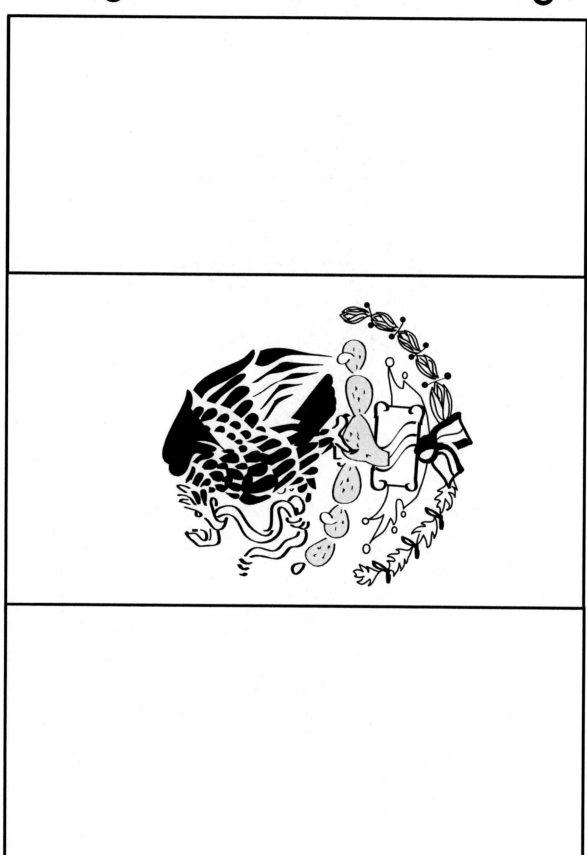

The Legend of the Mexican Flag *(cont.)*

The Poinsettia—a Mexican Treasure

Background Information

The legend of the poinsettia is a traditional Mexican story. It is a legend that tells of the origin of the beautiful poinsettia, the Christmas flower native to Mexico. In Mexico, this beautiful red flower grows abundantly, and can often be seen in patios and courtyards. Its bright red leaves form beautiful stars at the ends of the branches.

Although we see the beautiful red leaves as the flower, they are not the true flower. The flower of the plant is the tiny center of the red leaves. The leaves were used by the Aztecs as a red dye and as a medicine to lower fevers. The Indians regarded the flower as a symbol of purity, and it was highly regarded by Moctezuma or Montezuma, the king of the Aztecs. He would have poinsettias brought to him because they did not grow in the highlands around Mexico City.

Poinsettias can be seen growing very large in Mexico. The plants can grow to be ten feet tall, and are often seen in patios, courtyards, doorways, and sometimes in the wild.

Joel Roberts Poinsett introduced these plants into the United States in the 1820s. Poinsett was an ambassador to Mexico appointed by President Andrew Jackson. The name poinsettia was given to the plant by William Prescott, a historian and horticulturist, who was asked to give the plant a common name. He chose the poinsettia in honor of the man who had introduced the plant to the United States. The scientific name of the plant is Euphorbia Pulcherrima, which means "very beautiful."

The Aztecs called the plant Cuetlayochitl. In Peru and Chile, it is called the "Crown of the Andes." The plant has also been called the lobster flower and the flame leaf flower. In Mexico today, it is known as the Flor de Noche Buena, or Flowers of the Holy Night. We shall see why in the story, Legend of the Poinsettia.

The Legend of the Poinsettia

As Christmas Eve was approaching, a small village in Mexico was preparing for the holiday. In the church, the people were busy decorating and setting up the nativity scene. On the night of Christmas Eve, the people of the village would come to the church to present gifts to the baby Jesus.

A little girl who lived in the village was very sad because Christmas Eve was fast approaching, and she was very poor. She had no gift to give to the baby. She tried to think of things to take. First she thought of taking eggs, but her family needed the eggs to feed all of the children. Then she thought of taking some clothing, but there was no extra clothing in the poor house.

The night of Christmas Eve arrived and the village people were heading for the church to give their gifts. The little girl's heart was full of sadness as she walked toward the church, for she still did not have a gift to give.

She waited outside while all of the people of the village entered the church. She heard the music and knew that soon people would present their gifts. She did not know what to do as she stood alone in the darkness with tears on her face.

Suddenly, she heard a voice and turned to see a woman standing in the shadows. The woman had a shawl around her head, and she seemed to come from nowhere. "Why are you crying?" the woman asked.

"I have no gift for the baby Jesus, and it is Christmas Eve," the girl cried. "I don't have anything to give to him." She lowered her head with sadness.

"It really doesn't matter what your gift is," the woman said. "It is only important that it is a gift from the heart, and that it is given with love. Take anything, but give it with a glad heart."

The Legend of the Poinsettia *(cont.)*

The only thing that the girl could find was a bunch of weeds growing by the side of the road. She bent down and picked a bunch and held them in her arms. She looked at the woman, who just nodded her head.

The little girl walked into the church and down the aisle. She could hear people whispering. "Why is that girl bringing weeds to the baby Jesus?" But she kept walking forward and laid the armful at the foot of the manger. Then she shut her eyes to say a prayer, hoping that her gift would be a good one.

While her eyes were shut, she heard people in the church gasp. When she opened her eyes, she saw what they saw. The weeds had turned into beautiful, red flowers shaped like the Star of Bethlehem. She knew then that her gift had been accepted because it was given from the heart.

Those red flowers were the first poinsettias, and were known as the Flor de Noche Buena, the Flower of the Holy Night. Since that night they have been the traditional Christmas flower in many countries of the

Activities

Read *The Legend of the Poinsettia* retold and illustrated by Tomie dePaola (see bibliography) for another version of this tale. As with most folk tales, there are many different tellings of the story.

Have the students find out more about poinsettias on the Internet at this site: http://www.urbanext.uiuc.edu/poinsettia/

Ask students to write stories explaining the origin of other plants or animals.

Read *The Tale of Rabbit and Coyote* or *The Hummingbird's Gift* for other ideas. (See bibliography.)

Discussion Questions

1. Ask students what gift they think they would give to someone they loved if they had no money to spend.

2. Why is giving with love more important than spending a lot of money?

3. What makes a gift truly valuable to the receiver?

4. What was the best gift you ever received? Why?

Poinsettia Magnet

Materials

- poinsettia patterns (page 115)
- red and green flexi-foam, or felt
- scissors
- glue
- magnet strip
- small yellow buttons (for flower center)

Directions

1. Make copies of the poinsettia patterns and trace them onto cardboard.
2. Cut out several sets of patterns for the class to use.
3. Have the students trace the leaf pattern onto their red material and cut out five or six of the leaves.
4. Cut the circle out of the green material.
5. Assemble the flowers by gluing the red leaves to the green circle.
6. Let the glue dry.
7. Glue the yellow buttons in the center of the flower.
8. Glue the magnet to the back.

Send a copy of the story home with each child to share "The Legend of the Poinsettia," and remind the children that gifts should come from the heart and not from the pocketbook.

Poinsettia Magnet *(cont.)*

Poinsettia Pattern

The Day of the Dead

One of the major holidays of the Mexican calendar is the Day of the Dead, or Día de los Muertos. This is actually a three-day celebration that involves food, music, family, and flowers. The holiday is a blending of the ancient Aztec traditions and the Catholic traditions that were introduced by the Spanish conquistadors. The Day of the Dead is often equated to our Halloween because both holidays fall at the same time of the year, but the Mexican tradition is much different in attitude and beliefs.

The most important thing to remember about the Day of the Dead is that it is not a scary or sad time. Even though the dead are welcomed back by the traditions, it is to celebrate and enjoy the company of the living. For the living, it is a time to welcome the spirits and memories of loved ones who have died. It is a time of celebration and reflection. Another thing to remember is that it is a holiday with a very long and involved history, and is therefore celebrated in different ways throughout the country of Mexico.

The holiday is divided into the following days:

- October 31 – All Hallow's Eve
  This is the night that the spirits of children who died come back to visit.

- November 1 – All Hallow's or All Saints Day
  This is a day to pray for the innocent souls of saints, martyrs, and children.

- November 2 – All Soul's Day
  This is a day to remember and pray for the souls of sinners.

The days before the holiday the markets are full of items needed to prepare the traditional foods and decorations. Skeletons and skulls are a common feature. The skeletons are usually comical figures doing everyday types of activities such as playing a guitar or dancing. Small sugar skulls are decorated with colorful icing, sequins, and other decorations. The names of children are often written on the sugar skulls, and they are treats much like Easter candy. The purpose of the skulls and skeletons is to make light of death and show no fear of it.

Bright yellow marigolds and deep red cockscomb are the flowers of choice for decorating the graves of the dead and the altars in the homes. In some areas, poinsettias are used. Families spend the day together making the gravesites of the departed, beautiful, with flowers, candles, small skeletons, and items that the dead enjoyed in life.

At home, the families will often build ofrendas, or altars, on which they will put a picture of a departed family member along with the things that that person most liked to eat or enjoy.

The Day of the Dead *(cont.)*

A typical ofrenda would have a picture of someone's grandmother, a bowl of fruit, a favorite drink, maybe a chicken leg or sandwich. Around all of this would be candles, flowers (marigolds and others), and possibly skeletons depicting an activity that that person enjoyed in life. The ofrendas range from fairly simple to quite ornate. Sometimes there are competitions in which the ofrendas are judged and given awards.

During each night of this holiday, families will go to the cemeteries to sit by the graves of the dead and contemplate their lives. The graveyards become filled with scents of flowers, candles, and copal incense. The cemetaries are brightly lit by hundreds of candles that decorate the graves. Families take food and have picnic dinners through the night. The sound of singing fills the air as groups of people sing to guitars and accordions. No one expects to be sad as people celebrate life while honoring the memories of their ancestors.

On one of the days, the families will have a large traditional meal. This is the time to have special foods. Mole, a dark, rich sauce made from chilies and cocoa, is a traditional dish for this time. Tamales and tortillas, chocolate and atole (a hot Mexican drink made from water, cornmeal and sugar) are also special favorites. One of the favorite traditional foods is the Day of the Dead bread.

Day of the Dead bread is called pan de muerto in Spanish. The bread is seen and sold everywhere during the holiday season. This special bread is made in rounded loaves topped with small figures of saints and skeletons. Sometimes the bread is molded into the shapes of people and animals. Often the bread is decorated with designs of colored icing. (See the activity on page 119 for making pan de los muertos.)

After all of the holiday preparations are completed, the people of Mexico enjoy the magic and mysterious Days of the Dead.

Discussion Questions

1. How does the Day of the Dead compare to our Halloween? What traditions are similar?

2. How does making an *ofrenda* compare to putting up a Christmas tree?

3. Which part of this holiday would you like best?

4. Which part of this holiday would you not like?

Suggested Reading

Pablo Remembers by George Ancona

A Gift for Abuelita by Nancy Luenn

The Spirit of Tío Fernando by Janice Levy

An Ofrenda for the Day of the Dead

Here is a picture of an ofrenda that someone might have in their house. The ofrenda is decorated with large orange flowers and food. Decide what food you might want to put on the ofrenda for your house. Draw the food you would have, and color the rest of the picture in bright, festive colors.

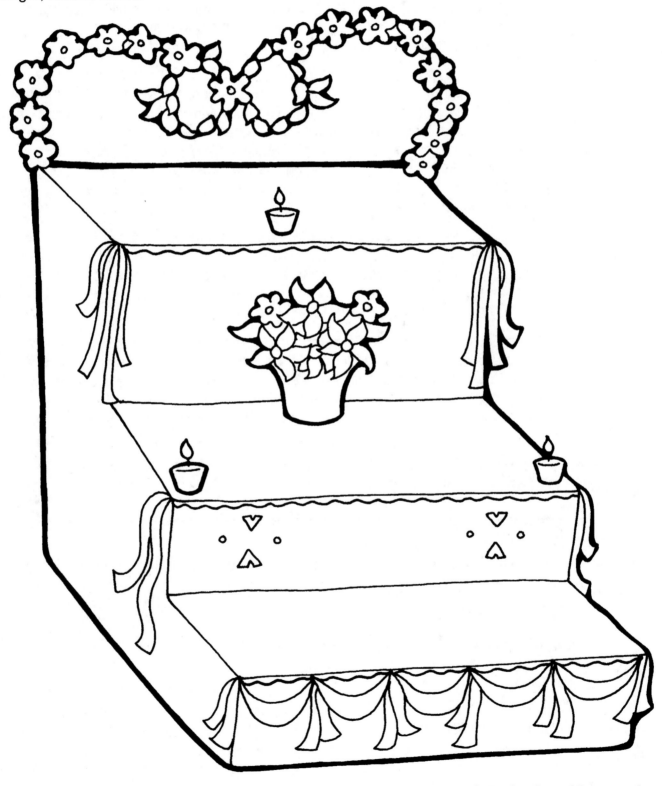

Treats for the Day of the Dead

Pan de los Muertos (Bread of the Dead)

Ingredients

- ½ oz. (14 g) active dry yeast
- 2 tsp. (10 mL) sugar
- ½ c. (120 mL) warm water
- ½ c. (100 g) butter
- 4 tsp. (20 mL) anise seeds
  (optional if you like the flavor of licorice)

- 12 c. (metric) sugar
- 1 tsp. (5 mL) orange flavoring
- 4 tbsp. (60 mL) orange peel
- 1 tsp. (5 mL) salt
- 2 eggs
- 5 c. (1 kg) flour

Glaze Ingredients

- ½ c. (100 g) sugar
- juice from one orange

Directions

1. To prepare the bread, dissolve in a large bow the yeast and 2 tsp. (10 mL) sugar in ½ c. (120 mL) warm water. Let this mixture sit for 5 minutes.

2. Scald milk and add anise seeds (if desired) over medium heat. Add sugar, butter, orange peel and flavoring, and salt. Warm ingredients until the butter melts. Let cool until lukewarm.

3. Beat eggs into yeast mixture. Stir in flour gradually to form a dough ball.

4. Next, knead the dough on a floured board until it is smooth and flexible. Reform into a ball and place in a mixing bowl. Cover and allow to rise until it doubles in size.

5. An hour or so later, preheat your oven to 350° F (180° C), and punch the bread down and knead for a few minutes.

6. Form the bread into a ball for the head, body, and longer shapes for the arms and legs. Attach these to the middle section. Depending on the size, 5 to 10 panes (little breads) can be made in the shape of children. You will need to double or triple the recipe for larger classes.

7. Place the little figures on a baking sheet, and let them rise for another hour. Then bake for 30 minutes or until slightly golden.

8. You may choose to make an orange glaze by heating the juice and 1/2 c. (100 g) sugar until thickened. Brush the glaze on the bread while it is still warm.

9. After the breads have cooled, use small tubes of colored icing to add faces and clothing.

Alternate Ideas

Make gingerbread cookies, but substitute ginger for the orange flavoring and let the children decorate their own cookies.

Buy bread dough or rolls and glaze before baking. Then decorate with icing or sugar crystals.

Music,
Arts,
and
Crafts

Huichol Art

The Huichol Indians from the states of Jalisco and Nayarit live in the western range of the Sierra Madre Mountains. It is a rugged area and not easily accessible to most tourists. For this reason, their traditions have changed little because of their isolation.

The Huichol people are descendants of the Aztecs and related to the Hopi Indians of Arizona. They have also kept their own religion and added portions of the Catholic religion. They have great respect and appreciation for birds, water, plants, the sun, fire, and rain. Their brightly-colored art is everywhere—on chairs, children's faces, bowls, and clothing.

They use these ideas from nature to create the plaques of yarn and beeswax which are called "faces or drawings of the world." They tell stories, ask for good crops and hunting, or are placed on altars as a thank you for their answered prayers. Nierikas made from various materials such as reeds or wool are pressed onto boards of warm beeswax. The Huichol also decorate gourds with colored beads, seeds, small pebbles, or kernels of corn by placing them in beeswax. They use them as gifts of thanks so that the prayers will be "drunk in." These prayer bowls are often placed in caves as offerings.

The Huichol Indians take small objects and tie them to a shaft, which is a stick with an arrowhead on the other end. These are driven into the ground to ask for special prayers. This is where the tsikuri or God's Eyes got their beginning on the shafts of wood or bamboo. They also called them prayer arrows. The colored yarns are wrapped around the wooden crosses. The Huichol believed the gods could watch their people through these and protect them, hence, the name God's Eyes evolved. These are placed in the hair of their children for their protection and are worn at the "Feast of the Ripe Fruits" to ask for good health and a long life.

The art of the tsikuri, nierikas, or decorated gourds is an important way for the Huichol Indians to pay honor to their deities and thus enable nature to be favorable to their land.

Discussion Questions

1. Which religious groups in the United States have kept their own traditions without much change since the 1800s?

2. What type of art does your temple, mosque, or church have?

3. What does it represent?

4. Have the students try these activities: face painting, yarn painting, and God's Eyes.

Yarn Painting

Materials

- 4" to 6" (10 cm x 15 cm) piece of cardboard
- scissors
- glue
- yarn
- pencil

Directions

1. Before beginning, talk with your students about the things for which they are thankful: a pet, food, their families, or something else important to them. Have them each draw one of these on their piece of cardboard.

2. Begin in the center and add glue thinly to a small area. Let the glue dry a little so that it is tacky to the touch.

3. Begin applying the first color by pressing the yarn onto the glued area and winding it as if you were traveling down a road. Have your students keep the rows of yarn next to each other so that the cardboard doesn't show.

4. After the artwork has dried, punch two holes in the top and tie yarn so the pictures can be displayed.

5. Have the children share why they chose their particular animal, person, or object to illustrate.

The pictures on the following pages are examples of traditional Huichol pictures that can also be used to do yarn painting. Students can glue copies of these pictures to cardboard and complete the yarn painting process.

Traditional Huichol Art

Traditional Huichol Art *(cont.)*

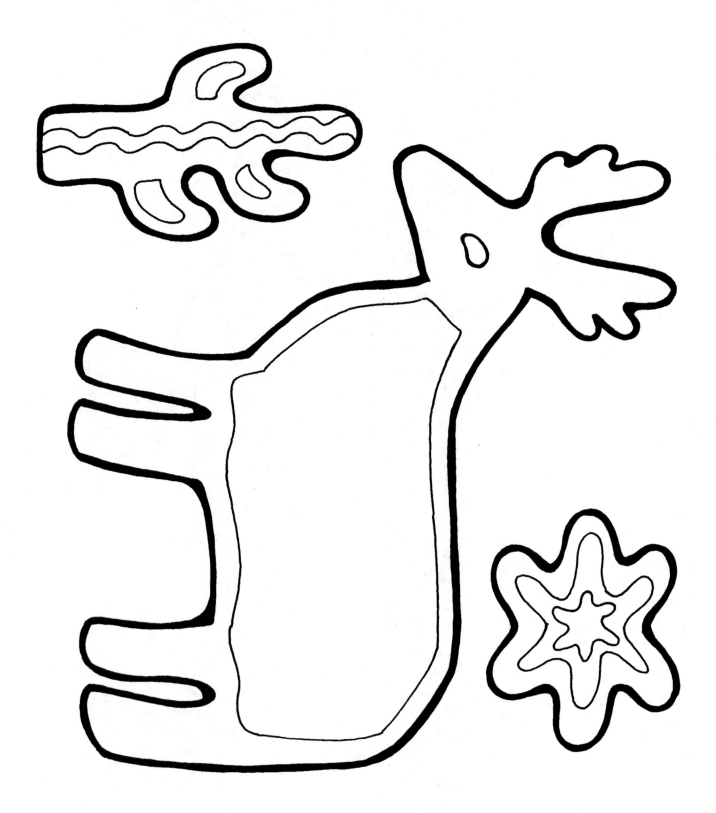

God's Eyes

Materials

- yarn
- scissors
- 2 craft sticks, tooth picks, or coffee stirrers
- glue

Directions

1. Glue two sticks together to form a cross.

2. Let the glue dry thoroughly.

3. Tie the yarn around the center of the cross to hold it in place. Younger children may need some help with this.

4. Begin wrapping the yarn around the cross alternating over and under each stick. Keep moving around it in a circle until you have the amount of color you want.

5. Colors can be changed by cutting and knotting on a new piece of yarn. For young children it is easier to buy a skein of yarn that is variegated with many colors.

6. After the wrapping is completed, tassels can be added to the ends of the crosses. Make the tassels by wrapping yarn around a piece of cardboard or several fingers a dozen times. Carefully slip the yarn off, keeping the loops intact. Tie one end of the loop to the stick and cut the other end so that the tassel hangs freely.

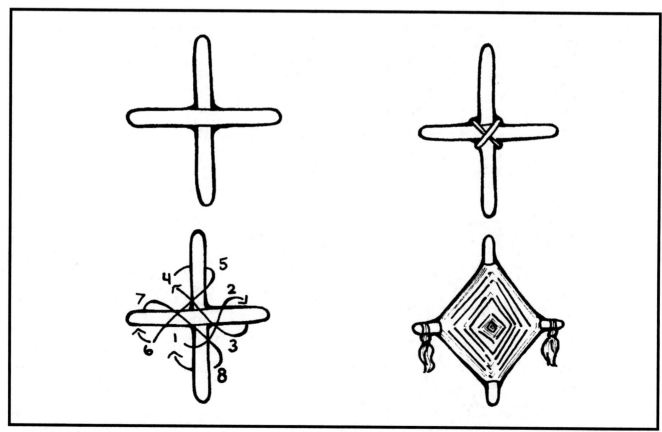

God's Eye Life Necklace

The Spanish name for God's Eyes is Ojo de Dios (oh-ho day dee-ose). In some Indian cultures, when a child is born, the father or other relatives will make the child his or her own ojo. It is usually white to symbolize the purity of the child. As the child grows older, colors are added to represent the happy or sad times of the child's life. When the child reaches the age of twelve, the special necklace is given to him or her as a remembrance of his or her life.

Discuss with the class what colors you would use to represent happy or sad times in your life. Why would you pick those colors?

Use the God's Eye pattern to make a small one for a necklace. You can use toothpicks and thread or dental floss for your string. This one should be your life necklace. Make the center in white, then add colors to represent important things that have happened to you. Small things might only need one or two threads, while bigger events might need several wrappings.

Events that you might include could be:

- a favorite birthday party
- starting school
- the loss of a friend or family member
- getting a pet

Remember to choose a new color for each event. Glue the ends of the strings to the toothpick.

After you finish your necklace, you can add small beads or shells and put it on a string long enough to wear around your neck.

Share with your classmates the story that your necklace tells about you. Explain to them why you chose the colors that you used.

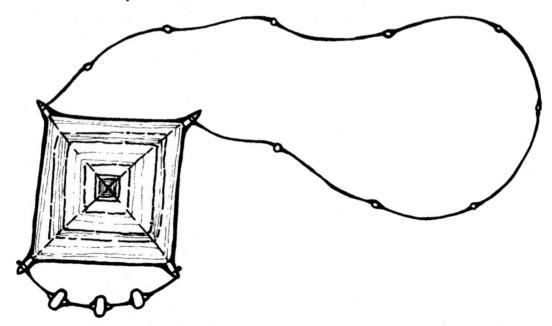

God's Eye Christmas Trees

God's Eyes make wonderful, colorful decorations for Christmas. They can be made in traditional Christmas red and green, or they can be made in bright fiesta colors. Use silver and gold metallic threads to add extra Christmas glitter. Embroidery floss comes in a rainbow of colors and often in shiny, satin-like finishes. Variegated threads and floss make interesting patterns, too.

Have the students make small God's Eyes to hang on a classroom Christmas tree. They can add beads and small buttons to the God's Eyes after they are finished. A large yellow or gold God's Eye can be put at the top of the tree for a star.

If you do not have room for a classroom tree, put a large construction paper tree on the bulletin board and have the students hang their God's Eyes on it.

The students can take their Mexican Christmas decorations home to give as holiday gifts and to share with their families.

Face Painting

Materials

- water-soluble paints
- brushes

Directions

1. Choose some simple designs from nature such as flowers, the sun, stars, snakes, or birds. Draw them on a large piece of cardboard.
2. Have each child choose his or her own favorite.
3. Paint the design on the face of each child.

This is a fun activity for special events at school, or for the Mercado activity.

Mexican Pottery

The pottery of Mexico is famous around the world. Mexican markets and shops sell pots and vases in bright colors. Some of the pottery includes little animals and figurines. Oaxaca is one state that is famous for its pottery.

In the town of Coyotepec, Oaxaca, potters make a famous blackened pottery. This pottery tradition was kept alive by Dona Rosa. Today her shop is still in operation where visitors can see the son of Dona Rosa making pottery using ancient techniques. This famous black pottery is made from special clay and then is fired deep within firepits in the earth for long periods of time.

More colorful pottery figurines are made by the famous Aguilar family. Their well-known work in pottery is completed in their home. The figurines depict people involved in everyday activities and more fanciful figures that inspire imagination. Their workshop is a place where the family lives, eats, and works.

Provide as many examples of Mexican pottery as you can find. The book *Oaxacan Ceramics* by Lois Wasserspring is an excellent source of pictures and inspiration. The photographs by Vicki Ragan are a wonderful way to inspire young potters with figures of mermaids, octopus, lizards, and saints.

Making pottery is a fun activity for students. On the next page are some whimsical designs that can be made from modeling clay. Students can have fun with the designs and should be encouraged to use bright colors in their work.

To make kiln-dried pottery, each student should have about ¼–½ pound (100 g – 225 g) of red clay. The centers of the pieces should be hollowed out (like Halloween pumpkins) so that the pieces will not explode in the kiln. Arms, legs, and other appendages should not be thicker than 1" (2.54 cm). Appendages can be added to the sculpture by making "slip," a paste-like mixture of clay and water. Score the areas that are to be attached with a fork, then apply the "slip" and allow to dry. After the pieces dry, the students can paint them with bright colors. Acrylic paint is best for this process.

Students can display their work around the room or at the *mercado*.

Mexican Pottery Animals

Mexican Pinch Pots

Pottery has been made and used throughout Mexico and Central America since ancient times.

Show some ceramic examples to the class or visit a company where pottery is made. Bring in some examples of Mexican pottery so students can study the modern designs and colors. Have the students research the history of pottery in Mexico, and some of the historical and traditional patterns and colors. For what did they use their containers?

Materials:

- self-hardening or oven-firing clay
- small containers of water
- brushes
- acrylic glazes, paints, or reddish-brown tempera paint
- spray acrylic sealer

Directions:

1. Give each student a ball of clay 2 or 3 inches (5 or 7.5 cm) in diameter.
2. Prepare the clay by throwing it down on a hard surface, and then kneading out the air bubbles. This is called wedging. Repeat this several times.
3. Pat and smooth the clay into a ball. Push both thumbs together into the middle. Shape the bowl by pulling the sides out from the center and pinching with the fingers. Be careful not to pinch the sides too thin. Turn the bowl frequently so that the sides remain the same thickness.
4. When you have a shape you like, dip your fingers into water to smooth out any cracks. Let the pot dry for several days or follow the manufacturer's directions to oven fire it.
5. Paint a base coat with a reddish-brown acrylic or tempera paint. When that coat is dry, paint a design similar to the examples of Mexican pottery, using a second color. Spray the finished piece with a ceramic sealer or lacquer.

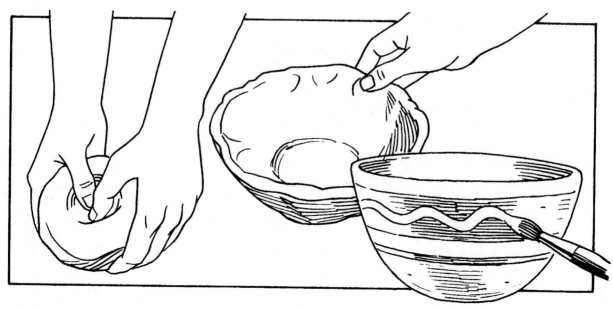

Papel Picado

On special occasions in Mexico, colorful banners are hung much like we use crepe paper. The banners are called *papel picado,* which means pierced paper. Traditionally, *papel picado* is cut from tissue paper, but now metallic paper is also being used.

You may choose to use tissue paper, but copy paper will work well and does not tear as easily.

Materials

- 8" x 8" (20 cm x 20 cm) squares of colored paper (16"x 16" [40 cm x 40 cm] will work well for larger ones)
- scissors
- string or thread

Directions

1. Fold the paper in half.

2. Fold in half again.

3. Have the children imagine two triangles on their papers, and fold diagonally so that the folded edges meet folded edges and open edges meet open edges. If they cannot hold the paper folded while they cut, have them use a paper clip or clothespin.

4. Explain that one edge has folded edges and one edge is the outside of the paper. They will begin by cutting a wavy edge along the outside of the paper. This will give their banner an interesting edge when it is finished.

5. Snip out shapes along the other two folded sides of the triangle.

6. Unfold the paper and see your beautiful papel picado.

7. Hang the banners around the room for a cheery Mexican fiesta! Use these to decorate the *Mercado.*

1.

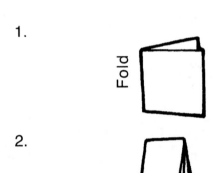

2.

3.

4.

5.

6.

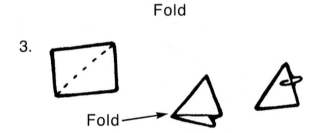

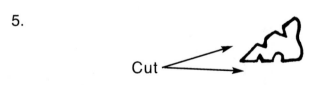

Mexican Blankets and Ponchos

Preparation

Explain to the students that weaving is an important occupation in Mexico. For many hundreds of years, Mexican people have woven blankets, rugs, ponchos, and other necessities. Today, many people still do hand weaving. (*Mexico the Culture* and *Mexico the People* both have pictures of people engaged in weaving.)

1. Collect pictures of Mexican rugs, ponchos, and other textiles for the students to look at and share. Try to choose colorful pictures showing patterns used by people in different sections of the country.

2. Locate some actual woven pieces to bring to class so that students can feel the textures and see the weaving. Ask the students for ideas about other things that are woven such as baskets and the clothing they wear.

Materials

- white or colored paper approximately 54" x 25" (135 cm x 65 cm) for each student or team
- strips and pieces of paper in a variety of bright colors
- glue
- scissors

Directions

1. Give each student the opportunity to choose a rug pattern that he or she likes.

2. Give each student a large sheet of paper.

3. Each student cuts the colored paper and pastes it onto the large sheet to make his or her own Mexican rug. Allow lots of room for creativity and self expression.

4. Have the students cut fringe along the ends of their rugs to simulate the fringed edges typical of Mexican weavings.

Suggested Activities

1. Exhibit the students' blankets by displaying them on the walls of the hallways.

2. You can make the blankets into ponchos by cutting holes in the center for student's heads. The students can then wear the ponchos around the school and have a Poncho Parade for the other students.

3. Students can also save their ponchos to wear at the *mercado* at the end of the unit.

Mexican Fiesta Place Mats

This activity gives students the opportunity to learn the basics of weaving. Students will also have a beautiful mat to use at the *mercado*, or give as a gift.

Preparation

Use the same preparation as for Mexican Blankets and Ponchos.

Materials

- 18" x 12" (46 cm x 30 cm) sheet of construction paper (background color)
- 16 strips of construction paper 1" x 12" (2.54 cm x 30 cm) (accent color)
- scissors
- glue
- ruler
- pencil

Directions

1. Fold the large sheet of paper in half widthwise.

2. Lay a ruler along the folded edge and mark the paper at each inch mark. Do the same along the opposite (open) edge.

3. Measure 1" (2.54 cm) up from the open edge and draw a line across.

4. Draw straight lines from the fold marks to the edge marks.

5. Starting at the folded edge and cutting through both layers, cut along the lines. Be careful to stop 1" (2.54 cm) from the edge of the paper. This edge holds your loom together.

6. Unfold the paper. This is your loom.

7. Weave the 1" (2.54 cm) strips through the loom.

8. Glue the ends of the strips to the edges of the loom.

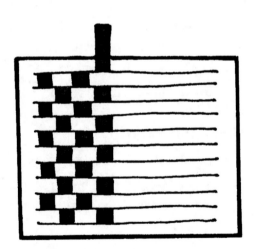

An easy way to make the 1" (2.54 cm) strips is to fold a piece of 9" x 12" (23 cm x 30 cm) construction paper lengthwise. Mark every inch along the open and the folded edges. Join the marks with straight lines. Cut along the lines all the way across the paper.

Allow students to experiment with color combinations. Let students try cutting the loom with wavy lines for an interesting optical effect.

Masks

Every region of Mexico has a village where masks are made. Masks have been an important art form in Mexico since the early days of its history. Frequently, masks are discovered in archeological sites dating back as far as 1600 B.C.

Masks were used in ancient cultures as part of the shamans' costumes. Masks were believed to protect people from danger and evil. Now masks are part of fiestas, carnivals and costume parties. The owl mask on the following page is popular with children in Puebla during carnival time.

During the Day of the Dead celebrations, people make masks that look like *calaveras*, which are skulls. You may want to make a *calavera* mask for your Day of the Dead celebrations.

Masks in Mexico are carved from wood, made of papier-mâché, or sometimes fashioned from cloth. Some of the ancient masks were made from stone, jade, or metal.

Materials

- poster board
- string
- scissors
- crayons or markers

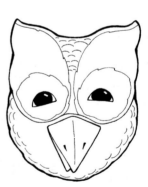

Directions

1. Reproduce the masks from pages 137–138 on poster board or heavier paper.

2. Have the students color the masks and cut out the eyeholes.

3. Attach strings to the masks so the students can tie the masks in place.

4. Students can wear their masks on a short mask parade around the school.

5. Students can wear, display, or sell their masks at the *mercado*.

Extension Activities

Three-Dimensional Mask

1. Give each student two copies of the owl mask on page 138.

2. Have them color the eyes, beak, and eyebrows on one of the masks and cut them out.

3. Glue the cut-out parts to the other mask and finish coloring. This will give the mask a three-dimensional look.

4. Have students complete the activities on page 136.

Masks *(cont.)*

Mask Math

1. Decide whether you would rather be an owl or a monkey. (Put on the mask of the animal you chose.) Why did you choose the animal you did?

2. If you are a monkey, stand on the north side of the room. If you are an owl stand on the south side.

3. Now think of a math statement about the number of students who chose to be owls compared with the number who chose to be monkeys. Share your idea with the class.

   Example

   Three more students are monkeys than are owls.

   If two people changed masks, would the sides be even?

4. Using the background below, draw a picture of your own owl and monkey math statement. Write the math statement below your picture.

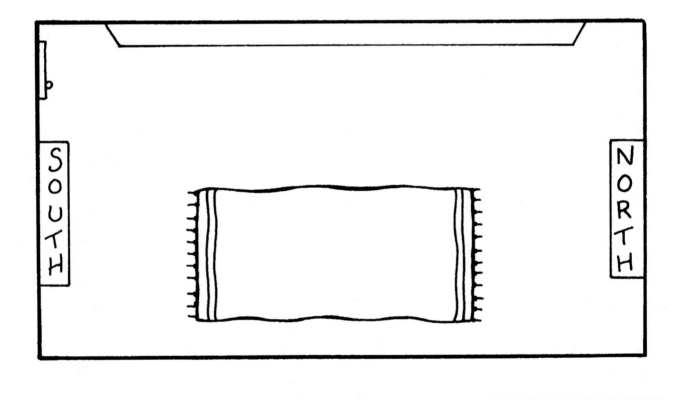

_____

_____

_____

_____

Masks *(cont.)*

Monkey Mask

Masks (cont.)

Owl Mask

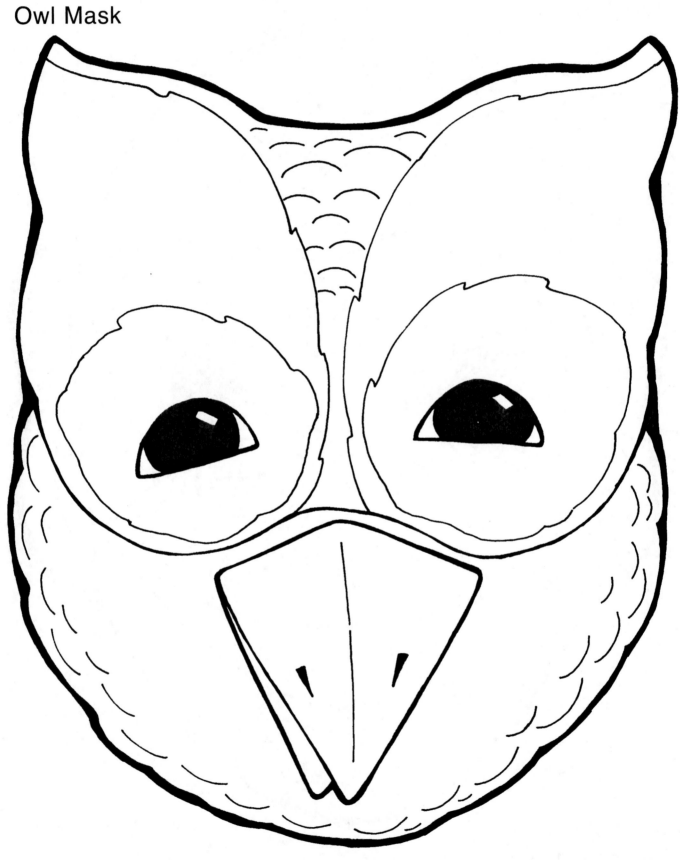

Musical Mexico

Music is very important in Mexico. Everywhere you go you hear music. Music is part of every fiesta, every holiday, and just about every day. Musicians wander around the parks and play their instruments for people. Bands play in the parks in the evenings, and it is common to see people dressed in brightly colored costumes dancing traditional dances.

One type of traditional music group in Mexico is called a mariachi band. Mariachi bands are very common, and often play at fiestas, birthday parties, weddings, and in restaurants. You may have seen a mariachi band if you have been to a Mexican restaurant. These bands usually have six to eight members. There are usually a violinist, a guitarist, a trumpeter, a singer, and a person playing a large instrument that looks like an overgrown guitar. Sometimes the group will have a harp or a bass. Occasionally you will see one with marimbas. The members of the group dress alike in traditional mariachi clothes that often include lots of silver decorations and large sombreros (hats). Mariachi bands are often men, but there are women mariachi bands also.

Another type of music group is called norteños or rancheros. The music sung by these singers is very popular in Mexico. It sounds a little like country western music. A norteño group will include an accordion, a guitar, and a singer who keeps time with a set of rhythm sticks.

It is fun to listen to music from other countries. Go to your library and see if it has tapes or CDs of traditional Mexican music. Check them out and listen to the music. Even if you don't understand the words, you will be tapping your feet. Play along with the music with your maracas or with castenets or by just tapping two pencils together.

The Mexican Hat Dance

The Mexican Hat Dance is a fun and easy dance to do. It is a traditional dance in Mexico, originally coming from the state of Puebla. It is easy to find the music for this dance.

How to do The Mexican Hat Dance

- Put a large sombrero in the center of the floor. If you do not have a sombrero, use a smaller hat, or draw a large chalk circle on the floor.

- Everyone stands around the edge of the circle with hands on hips. When the music starts, jump from one foot to the other in time with the music and clap your hands with each jump. When the music changes to the verse, promenade around the circle, linking arms with the others that you meet. Repeat the activity.

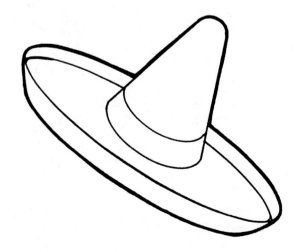

Mexican Bird Rattle

A popular tradition for New Year's celebrations and annual fiestas is the making of papier-mâché rattles. These joyful noisemakers are usually shaped to resemble colorful bird heads. The rattles are shaken to welcome generous spirits of the new year and to drive away any unhappy spirits remaining from the past.

Materials

- 9" (23 cm) stick or dowel
- cardboard toilet paper tube
- scissors
- feathers
- starch
- bowls

- glue
- pencil
- masking tape
- used file folder
- paper towels
- beans or small stones

- newspaper to cover work area
- paintbrushes
- tempera or acrylic paint
- patterns (page 141)
- aluminum foil (optional)

Procedures

1. Seal one end of the cardboard tube with masking tape.
2. Insert the stick into the open end and tape it in place.
3. Add beans into the tube and seal the end closed with tape.
4. Cut out a beak from the file folder and tape or glue it in place.
5. Tear short, narrow strips of paper towels. Dip them into the starch, and apply them on the rattle structure. Cover the entire rattle, except the handle, in this manner with two layers of paper towels.
6. Paint the rattle when it has dried thoroughly.
7. Glue features to the top of the head.

Variations

1. *Round Heads:* To make a round head for the bird, crumple aluminum foil and tape it around the cardboard tube.
2. *Tissue Paper:* Instead of paint, cover the head with bright colors of tissue paper. Tear small pieces and apply by using a paintbrush dipped into acrylic polymer or diluted white glue.

Mexican Bird Rattle *(cont.)*

Beak Patterns

Place dotted edge of each pattern on fold.

Papier-Mâché Maracas

A person who makes masks or toys from paper is called a cartonero. A cartonero keeps busy making figures for religious holidays or special celebrations like birthday parties. We know these figures as piñatas. Some of these figures are over ten feet tall and are carried in parades. These paper sculptures are made to last a short time, since, like the piñata, which is broken with a stick, they are often burned or exploded with fireworks.

During some fiestas in Oaxaca, young boys and some girls wear papier-mâché bulls, baskets and monkeys on their heads. Firecrackers are attached to the frames, and the wearers chase after people in the crowds as the firecrackers go off all around them. Surprisingly, few people are hurt by these activities, but it is still dangerous and should not be attempted.

Recycling materials is common in Mexico. People use old tires to make soles for their sandals and they use animal hair to make paintbrushes. Scraps of paper go into the papier-mâché for making helmets, swords, masks, piñatas, rattles, and other toys.

Materials

- scraps of paper brought in by the students
- small balloons
- material to make the rattling noise (beans or small stones work well)
- sticks or dowel rods 6"-10" (15 cm - 26 cm) (optional)
- flour paste

Directions

1. Prepare the flour paste by mixing 1 cup (240 mL) of flour with 2 cups (480 mL) of water.

2. Tear the paper into narrow strips.

3. Blow up the balloons.

4. Dip the paper strips into the paste.

5. Wrap the strips around the balloon, layering them to cover all of the balloon surface. Make sure that all of the balloon is covered except a small hole and that the paper is not too thick. The thicker the paper, the longer it will take for the balloons to dry.

6. Put the paper-covered balloons in a safe place to dry.

7. When the paper is dry, deflate the balloon and pull it out through a small hole.

8. Insert the beans or other rattle material into the hole.

9. If you want the students to have handles on the maracas, have them put the sticks into the hole and securely tape around them to steady them.

10. If the maracas are not going to have handles, just tape over the hole with masking tape.

11. Paint the maracas bright colors.

142

Singing in Spanish

Here are a couple of songs that you can learn to sing in Spanish.

This song is sung to the tune of "Are You Sleeping?"

Fray Felipe (fray fay-lee-pay)
Fray Felipe
¿Duermes tú? (dwer-mays too)
¿Duermes tú?
Toca la campana (toe-ka la kam-pan-a)
Toca la campana.
Tan, tan, tan. (taun, taun, taun)
Tan, tan, tan.

Translation

Brother Philip
Are you sleeping?
The bell is ringing.
Ding, ding, ding.

Here is a little game you can play. It is called "La Casa Del Conejo" (The Rabbit's House). Everyone stands in a circle except one person who stands in the middle. The person in the middle is the rabbit. Everyone chants the two verses, and at the end of the second verse, the rabbit picks another person to be in the center. Repeat the game until everyone has had a chance to be the rabbit.

Es la casa del conejo
Y el conejo no está aquí.
Ha salido esta mañana
Y no ha vuelto por aquí.
Ay, ay, ay, ay!
El conejo ya está aquí.
Escoge a la niña (niño)
Que to gusta más a tí.

Translation

This is the rabbit's house
And the rabbit isn't here.
He went out this morning
And has not returned here.
Oh, oh, oh, oh!
The rabbit is now here.
Choose the girl (boy)
That you like most.

Food
and
Fun
in the
Kitchen

Mexico's Food

Lots of people enjoy Mexican food. When we think of Mexican food, we often think of tacos, enchiladas, and nachos. Much of what we consider to be Mexican food is actually Tex-Mex, or food that comes from the southwestern United States. This tasty food is a mixture of traditional Mexican foods and American tastes.

Mexican food is not always hot. The food from the south of Mexico tends to be spicier than the food from the northern regions. Some dishes are found in only certain sections of Mexico, while others are found all over the country.

Mexico has always had a wide variety of native foods from which to choose. Tomatoes and corn were foods eaten by the Aztecs. Chilies and avocados have flavored Mexico's food for centuries. Lettuce, radishes, onions, pumpkins, and beans are essential to the Mexican cuisine. Limes, pineapple, and papaya are some of the popular tropical fruits.

Chicken is widely used in Mexico, and turkeys are frequently sold in markets. Beef, pork, and goat are included in many menu items. Cabrito, which is baby goat, is a specialty in the northern town of Monterrey. The long seacoasts provide large quantities of seafood including red snapper, sea bass, shrimp, and other fish.

Sauces are popular in Mexico. We are familiar with salsa, a mixture of tomatoes, chilies, and onions. Other popular sauces include guacamole made from avocados and seasonings. Mole (mo-lay) is a sauce used widely in Mexico. Different sections of the country pride themselves on their specific mole sauces, that can involve more than two dozen ingredients in the preparation. Chilies, herbs, spices, and chocolate are used in the making of this special sauce, often served on holidays. Mole poblano comes from Puebla; and in Oaxaca, mole making is a fine art. There is also a green mole made with pumpkin seeds.

An interesting snack food in Oaxaca is chapulines. Served from large platters, this reddish dish may look a little strange to you. It is fried grasshoppers!

Extension Activities

Obtain menus from some local Mexican restaurants. Share the menus with the children and discuss the ingredients. What are the foods they like best? What do they like least?

Have the students plan a trip to a Mexican restaurant. What would they order? How much does each item cost? How much money would they need in order to eat at that restaurant?

Discuss the similarities between some Mexican foods and traditional American foods. How are a taco and a sandwich alike? Why do you think such foods were invented?

Examine the Mexican menu and count the items that include corn or beans. Why would so many foods from Mexico include these two items?

Two Cool Watermelon Treats

In many parts of Mexico, the weather is very hot. People are always looking for cool things to eat and drink. The markets sell treats for people to eat while they are shopping.

One popular way to cool off on a hot day is to eat watermelon. Vendors on the streets will sell fresh, cool watermelon cut up into small cubes and served cold. For just a couple of pesos, you can have a refreshing treat.

In Mexico, watermelon is served a little differently. You can have your watermelon sprinkled with a little salt and lime juice. The salt and lime juice make the watermelon taste even sweeter and more refreshing.

Try it. You will like it on a hot summer day, and you can surprise your family and friends with a tasty new watermelon treat. You might even want to set up your own watermelon stand in your neighborhood next summer.

Ingredients

- watermelon cut into small chunks (seedless is nice)
- salt shaker
- small bottle of lime juice
- small plastic sandwich bags
- toothpicks

Directions

1. Put 8-10 chunks of watermelon in a plastic bag.
2. Sprinkle with a little salt and a few drops of lime juice.
3. Serve with a toothpick so your friends can eat right out of the bag.

The Spanish word for watermelon is sandía.

You can make a sign that says:

Se Vende Sandía – 1 peso

It means "Watermelon for sale—about $.10"

Two Cool Watermelon Treats *(cont.)*

Another cool way to serve watermelon is to make frozen watermelon fruit bars.

Ingredients

- watermelon cut into pieces that will fit into a blender
- a blender
- small paper cups
- craft sticks
- salt and lime (optional)

Directions

1. Put the watermelon into a blender and blend until smooth. The seeds will fall to the bottom of the mixture.
2. Add salt and lime juice if you wish.
3. Pour the watermelon juice into paper cups (leave the seeds behind) and freeze.
4. Put the craft sticks into the center of the cups when the mixture is frozen enough to hold them upright, but before the mixture is frozen solid.
5. Allow the cups to freeze solid.
6. Take off the paper cups and enjoy!

The Spanish word for a frozen fruit bar is palito.

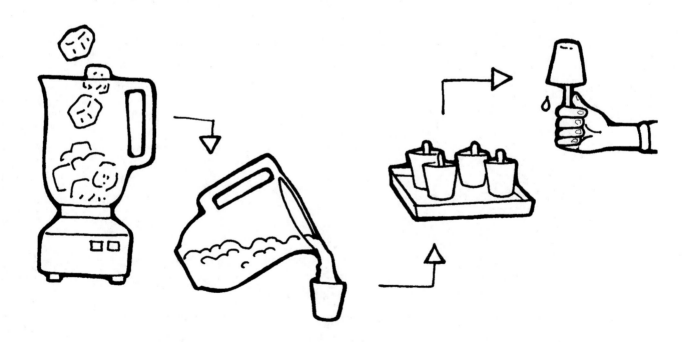

Chocolate Mexicano

Chocolate was one of the surprises that awaited the Europeans in the New World. The Aztecs were using chocolate when the conquistadors came. It was a favorite drink of the emperor Moctezuma (or Montezuma). The word chocolate is from the Aztec word chacolatl.

Ingredients

- 2 cups (480 mL) milk
- 1 oz. unsweetened chocolate squares
- 1 tbsp. sugar

- ½ tsp. cinnamon
- pinch of salt

Directions

1. Heat the milk and chocolate in a saucepan until the chocolate melts.

2. Add the spices, and whip with a beater. Use a molinillo if possible. (Molinillo— a hot-chocolate whisk.)

3. Beat until foamy.

4. Pour into a ceramic pitcher to serve.

You can substitute Mexican sweet chocolate for the unsweetened chocolate, sugar, cinnamon and salt. Follow the directions on the box.

The Chocolate Poem

As you make your chocolate, you may want to sing the song that Mexican children sing. This is also a game. Young children sing the song as they make the motions of stirring up the chocolate.

The proper way to stir the chocolate is to hold the handle of the wooden whisk (molinillo) between your hands and twirl it. This beats the chocolate into a foamy froth.

Pretend you are whipping the chocolate as you chant this poem.

Chant	Translation
Uno, dos, tres, cho	One, two, three, cho
Uno, dos, tres, co	One, two, three, co
Uno, dos, tres, la	One, two, three, la
Uno, dos, tres, te	One, two, three, te.
Bate, bate, chocolate! (ba-tay, ba-tay, cho-ko-la-tay)	Whip, whip the chocolate!

This is a fun chant to teach your friends and family!

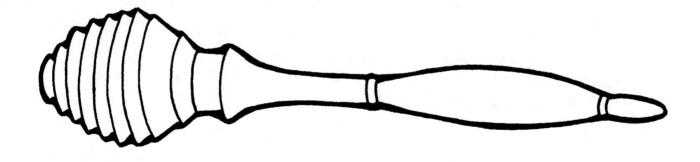

Nano's Trip to the Market

Había una vez . . .

Once upon a time there was a niño whose name was Nano. Nano lived with his parents in Oaxaca, Mexico.

One day Nano's mamá said, "Nano, I am going to make hot chocolate today because your abuelita is coming to visit, and you know how your grandmother likes chocolate. Go to the mercado and get the ingredients. I will need chocolate, leche, azúcar, and canela."

Nano loved the hot chocolate drink made with chocolate, milk, sugar, and cinnamon. He was happy to help.

"Sí, mamá," Nano replied. "I can do that!" he said proudly.

His mamá handed him enough pesos to pay for the chocolate, leche, azúcar, y canela.

"Now, Nano, can you remember what I need?"

"Sí, mamá the chocolate, leche, azúcar, y canela."

"Bueno. Now ándale, but first give me a hug." Mamá gave Nano un abrazo and dos kisses on each cheek.

"Adiós, mamá," Nano said as he left.

"Vaya con Dios, Nano."

Nano enjoyed walking through the town to the market. He liked the sights, the smells, and the noises.

Soon he heard some música and stopped to listen. The mariachi music was very lively and made him want to dance. But Nano remembered his job and thought, "I must hurry to get mamá the chocolate, leche, azúcar, y canela," and off he went.

Nano continued through Oaxaca to the mercado, and next he saw a man with a monkey. The monkey was dancing, and Nano thought he was very funny, so he stopped to watch. Then he remembered, "I must hurry to get mamá the chocolate, leche, azúcar, y canela," and off he went.

Nano's Trip to the Market *(cont.)*

Oaxaca has many colorful and interesting sights. On the next corner was a man painting pictures. The pictures had bright colors and Nano thought they were very pretty. He stopped to chat and admire the artist's work. Then he remembered, "I must hurry to get mamá the chocolate, leche, azúcar, y canela," and off he went.

A little further along, Nano saw a man carving an armadillo out of wood. Nano stopped to look at all of the brightly-painted carvings. "Qué bonito," he thought to himself. Suddenly he remembered, "I must hurry to get mamá the chocolate, leche, azúcar, y canela."

He entered the market and found the chocolate seller. He bought the chocolate, azúcar, y canela for his mamá. He paid the señora and said, "Gracias."

"De nada," responded the señora. "Adiós, Nano. Hasta pronto."

Next, Nano went to the lechería and got the milk. He paid the señor and said, "Gracias."

"De nada," answered the señor. "Adiós, Nano. Hasta luego."

Nano knew he must hurry home to keep the milk fresh. He hurried past the woodcarver and waved. He hurried past the artist and smiled. He hurried past the man with the monkey and laughed. He hurried past the musicians and their lively music and wanted to dance.

When Nano arrived home, he said, "Hola, mamá. Here is your chocolate, leche, azúcar, y canela."

"Gracias, mi hijito."

Mamá prepared the chocolate. She let Nano whip the chocolate into a beautiful foam with the molinillo.

Then Nano heard his abuelita knocking at the door and went to give his grandmother un abrazo.

Abuelito, Mamá, and Nano sat on the patio to enjoy their chocolate. Nano thought it tasted especially good since he helped by buying the chocolate, leche, azúcar, y canela.

Nano's Trip to the Market *(cont.)*

Vocabulary

Había una vez (a bee´ya oo´na base´)   **Once upon a time**

niño (neen´ yo)   **a young boy**

Mamá (ma ma´)   **mama, mommie**

sí (see´)   **yes**

abuelita (a bwa lee´ ta)   **dear grandmother**

mercado (mare ka´ doe)   **market**

chocolate (cho ko la´ tay)   **chocolate**

leche (lay´ chay)   **milk**

azúcar (ah zoo´ car)   **sugar**

y (ee)   **and**

canela (ka nay´ la)   **cinnamon**

bueno (bway´ no)   **good**

ándale (an´ do lay)   **hurry up**

adiós (ah dee ose´)   **good-bye**

vaya con Dios (bye´ ya con dee´ ose)   **go with God**

música (moo´ zee ka)   **music**

mariachi (mar ee aw´ chee)   **traditional street musicians**

qué bonito (kay bow nee´ toe)   **how pretty**

gracias (graw´ see us)   **thank you**

de nada (day naw´ da)   **you are welcome**

hasta luego (aws´ ta loo way´ go)   **until later**

hola (o´ la)   **hello**

hijito (ee hee´ to)   **little son**

patio (pat´ ee o)   **outside sitting area**

(Nano's Trip to the Market is an original story—copyright 1999 by Ann Greenman Barnell and Jane Carroll Routte.)

Mexican Recipes

Salsa

Ingredients

- 5 medium tomatoes
- ½ cup (100 g) cilantro leaves
- ½ tsp. chopped garlic
- 3 caps full of lemon juice
- Tabasco or jalapeños to taste

Equipment

large bowl for mixing

chopping board

knife for chopping

large spoon for mixing

Directions

1. Gather ingredients.
2. Wash and chop tomatoes. Put in the bowl.
3. Chop or tear cilantro leaves and add to tomatoes.
4. Add chopped garlic.
5. Mix all ingredients together.
6. Add lemon juice and mix lightly.
7. Taste.
8. Add tabasco sauce or jalapeños to taste.

This recipe has many variations. Instead of chopping the tomatoes by hand, you can put all of the ingredients into a food processor and mix. You can add more of any ingredient to make it taste the way you like it best. You may want to add a little salt. The texture of the salsa can be chunky or smooth depending upon how much you mix and stir it. Serve with corn chips or tortillas.

Mexican Recipes *(cont.)*

Galletas (cookies)

Mexican Wedding Cookies (Polvorones)

Ingredients

- 2 cups (450 g) flour
- ¾ cup (150 g) sugar
- ½ cup (100 g) chopped pecans
- 1 cup (225 g) butter
- small amount of powdered sugar

Equipment

mixing bowl

beater

spoon for mixing

ungreased cookie sheet

Directions

1. Preheat the oven to 300°F (150°C).
2. Sift flour and sugar together. Add the chopped pecans.
3. Cream butter and gradually mix in the flour mixture.
4. When all of the flour is mixed in, roll little pieces of the dough into balls and put them on the cookie sheet.
5. Bake for 25 minutes.
6. Sprinkle the tops of the cookies with powdered sugar.

154

Mexican Recipes *(cont.)*

Easy Cinnamon
Sopapillas

Sopapillas are a sweet dessert to serve at the end of your Mexican meal. They are also good to sell in the market place.

Here is an easy way that you can make sopapillas.

Ingredients

- one package of small flour tortillas
- ½ stick of butter (melted)
- 2 cups (480 mL) of cooking oil
- 1 tbsp. cinnamon
- ¼ cup (50 g) sugar

Directions

1. Mix together cinnamon and sugar. Set aside.
2. Heat the oil in a small but deep pan. Be very careful of the hot oil and make sure that an adult helps you with this.
3. Fry a tortilla until it is golden.
4. Have an adult take the tortilla out of the pan with tongs.
5. Lay the tortilla on paper towels to drain.
6. Brush the tortilla with melted butter.
7. Sprinkle the tortilla with the cinnamon and sugar mixture.

Eat and enjoy!

¡Deliciosa!

Mexican Recipes *(cont.)*

Quick Quesadillas

Queso (kay-so) is the Spanish word for cheese. Many Mexican dishes use cheese. You can find chili con queso (chilies with cheese) and just queso sauce (melted cheese for nachos and dips). Quesadillas are small Mexican "pies" with cheese in the middle.

Here is how you make these quick and easy treats.

Ingredients

- one package of any size of flour tortillas
- one package of grated cheese (grated cheeses come already mixed in Mexican flavors)

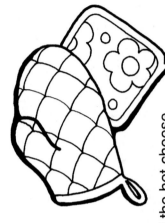

Directions

1. Place a small amount of cheese in the center of the tortilla.

2. Fold the tortilla in half.

3. Place it on a paper plate and cook for about 30 seconds in the microwave. Make sure that your cheese is melted. Be careful of the hot cheese.

4. If you do not have a microwave, you can cook these in an electric skillet or on the stove.

5. You can add all kinds of things to your quesadillas before you cook them. Some good things would be chilies, tomatoes, or cooked meat. Experiment and invent your own special Quick Quesadilla recipes!

These quesadillas make great, fast breakfast treats!

Mexican Recipes *(cont.)*

Homemade Corn Chips

Corn was one of the gifts of the new world. The native Americans used corn as a staple in their diet, and it is still very important in Mexico today. One of the most famous foods made from corn is the tortilla or corn chip, and it is included in most Mexican meals.

You can make your own corn chips by using this recipe.

Ingredients

- 1 cup (225 g) yellow corn meal
- 1 tbsp. of butter
- ¾ cup (180 mL) hot water

Directions

1. Lightly oil or spray an 11" x 15" (28 cm x 39 cm) jelly-roll pan.

2. Mix all of your ingredients in a mixing bowl and pour into the pan. Spread or shake the pan until the mixture is evenly distributed.

3. Bake in a 325°F (160°C) oven for 30–40 minutes until the corn mixture is crisp and comes away from the pan easily.

4. Sprinkle with salt to taste. Break it into pieces and enjoy with a dip or salsa.

The Market

El Mercado

The market place is the heartbeat of Mexico. It is the place where color, noise, scent, and sound come together. It is the meeting place, the bargaining place, the place where tradition and culture carry on. Going to the market is a central part of life in Mexico. It is often a day-long activity filled with bartering, buying, and eating. The markets offer food, clothes, and necessary items, along with fun and frivolous things.

The market is a great culminating activity for the Mexico unit. It will give your students the opportunity to display and share all of the aspects of Mexico that they have studied. The suggestions below will help you to make your Market Day a success.

1. Show pictures of Mexican markets to the children. (*Mexico, the People* or *Uno, Dos, Tres; One, Two, Three* or *Saturday Market*)

2. Read *Uno, Dos, Tres; One, Two, Three* or *Saturday Market* (see bibliography) to the class. Have students talk about how a market in Mexico would look, sound, and smell. What would be pretty? What would smell good? Who would be talking, and what things would they say?

3. Teach the concepts of being a good consumer. For example, waiting in lines patiently, speaking politely to others, and clearly asking for what they want to buy.

4. Teach the concepts of being a good vendor. For example, treat patrons with respect, charge correctly, give accurate change, and say thank you to the buyer.

5. Students should decide beforehand in which market booth they would like to work. Remember, one student should be in the bank and be in charge of handing out pesos to the other students. Determine a fair amount that the students will be allowed to draw from the bank. One idea is to have them sign for the money so they have the feeling of actually dealing with a bank.

6. Students can arrange the areas of the market by standing behind their tables, or by laying out their wares on blankets on the floor. They can use the paper blankets from **Mexican Blankets and Ponchos** on which to put their wares. Explain to them that in Mexican markets, many people sit on blankets to sell their wares. They can also wear their blankets as ponchos and use their placemats to display their wares.

El Mercado *(cont.)*

7. Enlarge the signs for the various booths on pages 168–174 and have the children color them. They could paste their signs to colorful construction paper. Remember, the more color, the better!

8. Have the children hang *papel picados* around the booths and the room. Hang the puzzles from Teamwork Activity around the room. Any other student work that has been completed during the unit should be displayed.

9. Play Mexican music in the background. Perhaps a small rhythm band would like to accompany the music.

10. Jobs at the Mercado:

Banco	Hands out the play money (see page 166) to students so that they can buy items in the market. This person is also responsible for collecting money from the vendors.
Tortillas	These can be as elaborate as the teacher wants to make them. Students can simply sell flour tortillas with butter on them, or they can make tacos with taco filling and cheese. Tortillas filled with cheese and microwaved become *quesedillas*.
Pan	The Mexicans borrowed heavily from the French in the making of their bread. If you do not have access to a Mexican bakery, then a loaf of French bread cut into slices and topped with butter or salsa will work well.
Chocolate	Use the chocolate recipe in the Food and Fun in the Kitchen section to make the drink for the class. Use the recipe as a math lesson so the children can figure out how much they will need to make to serve the class. The recipe makes two cups.
Doritos	Use the corn chips recipe to make chips, or buy taco chips at the store. Students can buy chips at one store and buy salsa at the other. This booth will need small plates or bowls.
Salsa	Use the salsa recipe to make salsa, or buy it ready-made at the store. Students can put the salsa on the doritos or the tortillas. Some may like it on the bread.
Galletas	The cookies can be the ones from the recipe in this book, or you can buy Mexican wedding cakes at the store. Any other cookie will work if Mexican cookies are not available. (Note: Mexican wedding cakes are called polvorones in Spanish. *Polvo* means dust or powder, since the wedding cakes are dusted with sugar.)
Frutas	Small dishes of cut-up fruit will work for this booth. Try to get fruits that came from Mexico, such as tomatoes, pineapple, avocado, coconuts, peanuts, sunflower seeds, etc. Students should be able to taste a little bit of each. The watermelon treats from this book would be a big hit.

El Mercado *(cont.)*

11. Students should share job responsibilities so that each student will be able to leave his or her booth and try the items from the other displays. This is a useful sharing and responsibility exercise.

12. All prices at the *Mercado* should be in even numbers so that there will not be a problem with making change. Stores should keep track of the money that they earn. A culminating activity will be for the class to compare the amounts of money earned by each store and make a chart of the highest earning store to the lowest.

13. Students can use their counting books to decide how much to pay for an item.

14. Storekeepers may make signs telling the prices of their items in Spanish, although in a real Mexican market the price is bargained between the buyer and the seller. You may want to encourage "bartering" with your class.

15. Students can recite songs they have learned, share their counting books, and show their increased knowledge of Spanish. Maps make good decorations for the walls.

16. Give students the opportunity to perform with maracas and participate in the Mexican hat dance.

17. Breaking a piñata would be a great finale to the occasion!

18. There are many possibilities for using this market activity in your classroom. It can be the way you choose to display the work that the students have done with the unit.

Invite as many guests as possible to your event. Parents, administrators, and community members love to attend this type of activity.

Have a great Mexican Market Fiesta!

Mercado Bingo

Mercado Bingo is a vocabulary game that helps students learn the names of items which they might find in a Mexican market. It is a useful preparation activity for having a *mercado* in the classroom, or it can be used independently to teach new words.

This game can be played in two ways. The students can hear the words and find the pictures on their cards, or they can see the pictures and find the matching word on their cards. The teacher can decide which is best for the class involved.

To prepare for the game, make copies of the blank game card (page 165). Make copies of the picture cards (page 163). Have the students color and cut out the pictures and glue them in random patterns to the blank game card, leaving the *gratis* (free) space open. As they work, have students name the items pictured. After they have finished making the cards, you might want to laminate them to use again.

If you want the students to match the pictures to the words, have them make game cards with the words cut out and pasted on the game cards.

This is a simple bingo-style game. Call out the names of the items, and have the students cover the pictures with buttons, pieces of corn, or bingo markers. Remember that the center space is free.

If you decide to have the students recognize the words, you will have to cut out the pictures and enlarge them so that the class will be able to see them. Coloring the pictures before or after enlarging them would be an enjoyable project for students.

Key	
pan	bread
frutas	fruit
chocolate	chocolate (in pitcher)
galletas	Mexican wedding cookies (on plate)
salsa	sauce (in bowl with tomato)
tortillas	tortillas
banco	bank (money)
doritos	chips

The rules are the same as for standard bingo. Students can win with straight lines up, down, or diagonally. Variations are four corners covered, or the entire card covered.

Make sure that the caller covers the words or pictures he or she has already used. The caller can pull cut words or pictures from a box.

Mercado Bingo *(cont.)*

Mercado Bingo *(cont.)*

Pan	Frutas	Salsa
Chocolate	**Gratis**	Galletas
Tortillas	Doritos	Banco

Mercado Bingo *(cont.)*

	Gratis	

Money for the Market

Uno
Peso 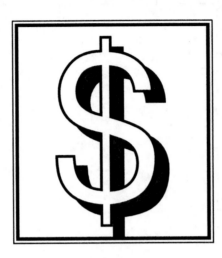 Mercado
Dinero

Cinco
Pesos  Mercado
Dinero

Diez
Pesos 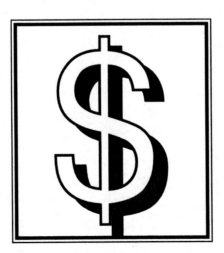 Mercado
Dinero

Parent Information Letter

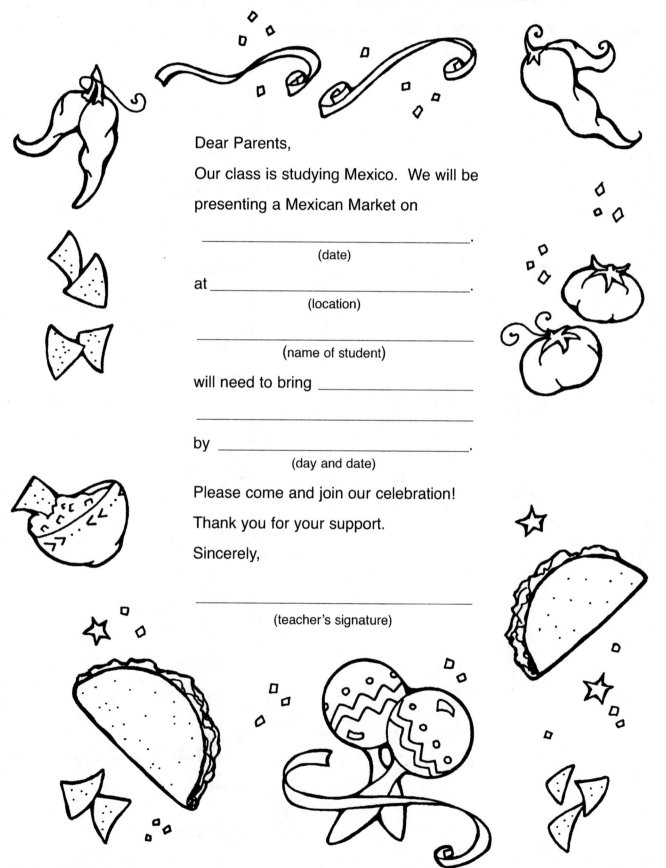

Dear Parents,

Our class is studying Mexico. We will be presenting a Mexican Market on

_____.
(date)

at _____.
(location)

_____
(name of student)

will need to bring _____

_____

by _____.
(day and date)

Please come and join our celebration!

Thank you for your support.

Sincerely,

_____
(teacher's signature)

Signs for the Market

El Mercado

Signs for the Market *(cont.)*

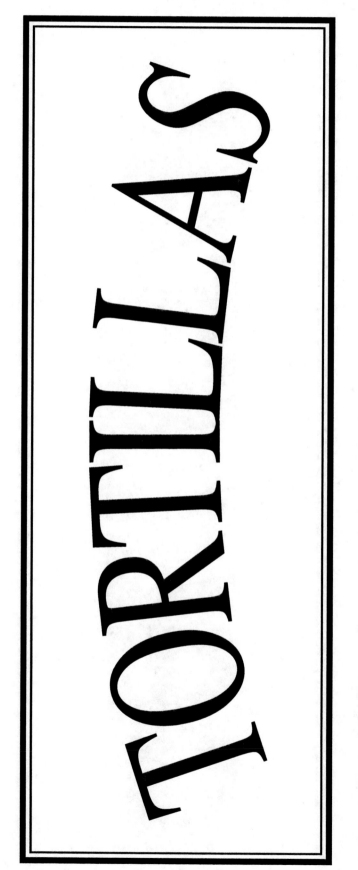

Signs for the Market *(cont.)*

Chocolate

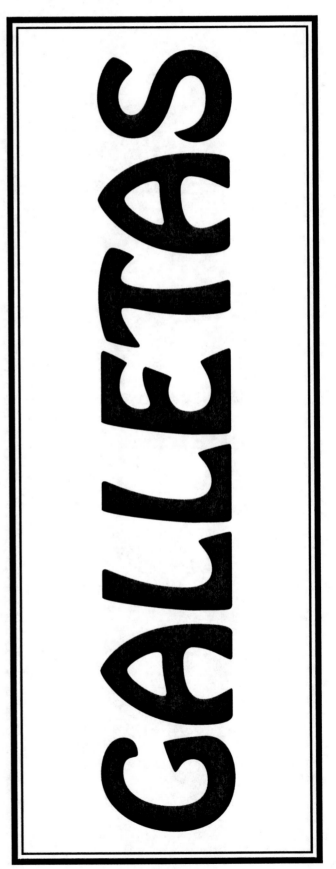

GALLETAS

Signs for the Market *(cont.)*

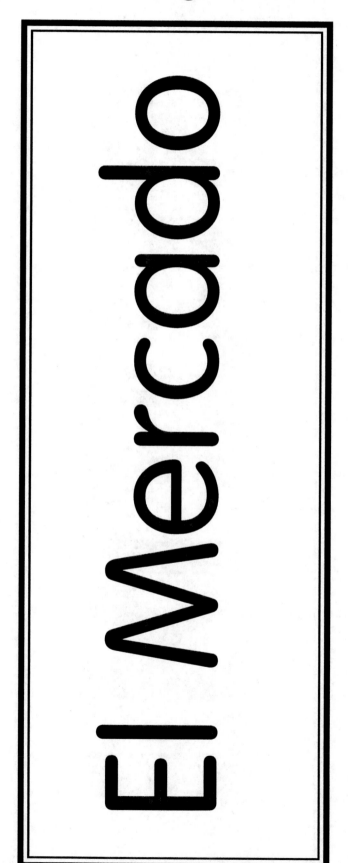

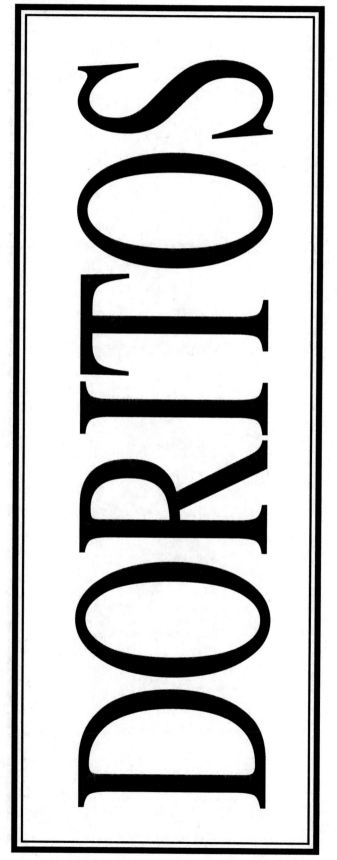

Signs for the Market *(cont.)*

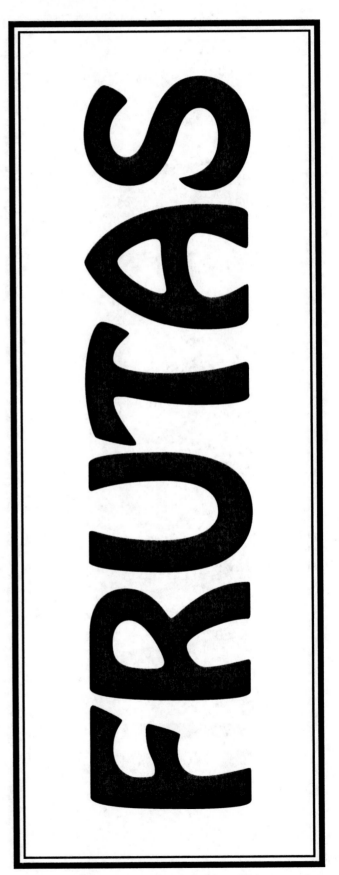

Signs for the Market *(cont.)*

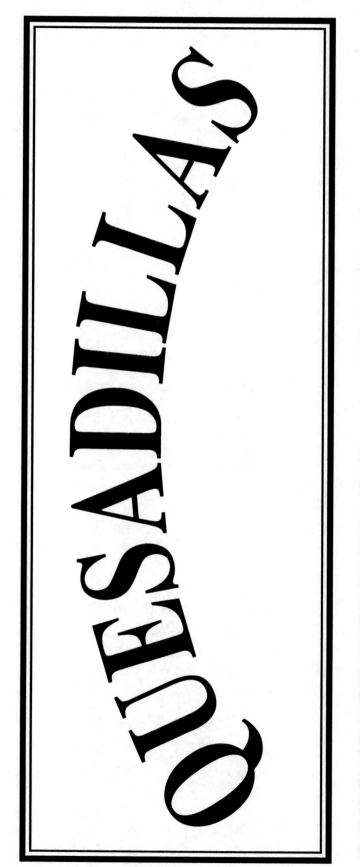

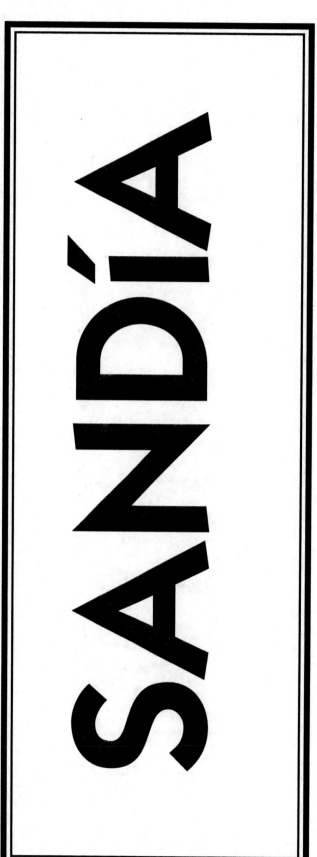

Signs for the Market *(cont.)*

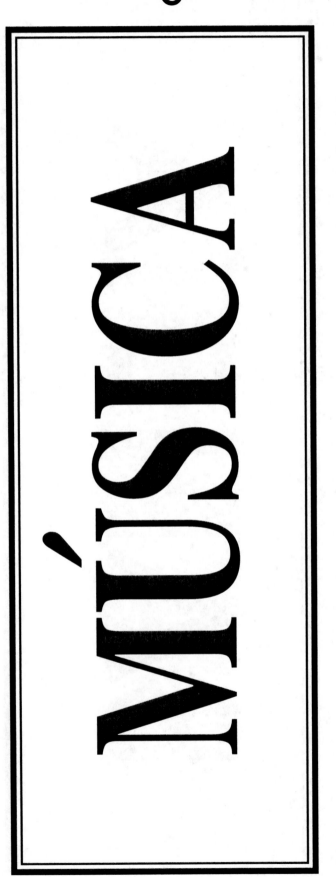

Citizen of the World Award

This award is presented to

_____

for completing our unit of study about

Mexico.

Congratulations on your achievement!

_____
(date)

_____
(teacher)

The Good Amigo Award

This award is presented to

_____

for being a good amigo in our class!

Good amigos do these things:

- follow class rules

- help others

- have a cheerful attitude

_____   _____
(teacher's signature)   (date)